Out the Window

43 Years on the Beat

Gerard Mulligan

outskirts
press

DEDICATION

This book is dedicated to all those newspaper columnists who have spent their lives sharing stories and observations. Pete Hamill, Art Buchwald, Jan Glidewell, Norm Swetman, David Arthurs, Lewis Grizzard, Steve Arthur, Carl Hiaasen, Mike Royko, and Dave Barry are just some of the names of those who kept me laughing for a lifetime.

Laughing is good for the soul. If we just read the headlines, we would cry every day.

Gerry Mulligan

ACKNOWLEDGEMENTS

There are many people who have helped me over the years in the newspaper business. I was one of those fortunate people who loved going to work every day. I made a living covering the news, producing newspapers and telling stories.

Just a few of those who helped along the way include David Arthurs, Greg Copeland, Jan Glidewell, Dick Morgan, Lucy Morgan, Jim Hunter, Tim Hess, Steve Arthur, Tom Saul, Mike Wright, Gary Chapman, Hampton Dunn, Dick Shelton, David Ernest, Garry Manning, Mike Arnold, Charlie Brennan, Chris Wessel, Dean Ridings, Ken Melton, Jim Twitty, Nancy Kennedy, Neale Brennan and George Wilkins.

Putting this book together was made easier by the assistance of Lori Hess, Trina Murphy, Tim Hess, Cindy Connelly, Jeremiah Mulligan, Tina Ruvalcaba, Hunter Mulligan and coffee.

My darling wife Janet has been my partner through it all.

TABLE OF CONTENTS

Chapter 1 - Sunday, Aug. 27, 1989

—◆—

THE LOGIC OF PADDLING IN
SCHOOLS FROM A PERSONAL VIEW

IT SEEMS THAT everyone has an opinion about paddling in the public school system.

Certainly, the majority of the people I speak with favor paddling in the school system. I don't doubt that many of you see children acting up at the grocery store or whining in a restaurant and contemplate that a good crack across the backside would probably help get that kid in order.

And I'll admit, I've been in enough social situations with children to appreciate the impact that a good spanking might have.

But I can't help think there's a time and place for everything; and having a teacher spank a disobedient child is a contradiction.

I'm sure it's my own upbringing that has soured me on the concept of paddling in the school system. I went to a Catholic grade school where we did not have physical education classes. Our teachers were all nuns and their only exercise for the week came from their daily paddling of students.

Now it may come as a surprise to many of you, but I received my share of paddling as a student. In fact, the first edition of a newspaper I ever worked for - editor of my grade school newspaper - resulted in a paddling.

It was an interesting form of censorship.

I certainly was more careful with my word selection with our second edition.

My fondest memory of abuse came in about the fifth grade when a lunchtime fist-fight erupted on the playground. While the good sister on duty attempted to break up the fight, some disgruntled future agitator disguised as a fifth-grader shouted a condescending remark to the teacher in question.

"Who said that," she demanded of the 300 students on the playground.

There was no answer.

"I insist that the culprit come forward immediately," the good sister roared.

No one moved.

Now if there was one thing Catholic school kids had, it was a sense of unity and honor. No one would turn in a fellow student.

"I want the guilty student to step forward or I will punish every one of you," the good sister demanded.

It seems a bit odd now, but at that time we had this rule that when a sister rang the bell, we were frozen in position until the next bell sounded. It would be hard to say that we were frozen on this day as it was June at mid-day in a very hot parking lot.

We stood there frozen, dripping sweat, wondering if any of the girls would turn Roy Plackus, the guilty fifth-grader, over to the now furious teacher. To their credit, the girls remained silent.

The good sister finally rang her second bell and sent all of the female students back to the class. She ordered all of the boys to stand in a straight line – alphabetical order, chests out, hands at our sides.

"This is your last chance," she demanded. "If you don't turn in the guilty party, every one of you will be punished."

Still no one said a word.

She then walked to the front of the line and began her attack. While the paddle was a weapon that existed in those days, the weapon of choice was a hand across the face.

A cold, fast hand directly to the cheek.

The first boy, that unlucky kid whose first name began with an "Ac," received a brisk blow to the face.

"This is your last chance," the good sister implored.

We would not relent.

She slapped through the A's with vigor.

She bumped through the B's with bounce.

She clubbed through the C's without compassion.

It was somewhere around the H's where she began to run out of steam. We had a lot of H's in those days. Hemsworths and Harringtons and Harmons.

I'm sure that it was somewhere in the H's where the good sister realized she still had another 110 boys to slap and that wasn't going to be an easy task.

We boys in the M's and N's began to gain in spirit. While she might make it to us, we knew the zip would be out of her zap.

It was at the L's where she finally gave up. She felt silly. I really believe she forgot why she was slapping in the first place. The heat was getting to her. We felt silly for her.

She stopped, said a few words in disgust, and marched back into the building. We stood out in the hot sun and some of us smiled. We didn't move for fear that a designated hitter might be coming over from the convent. But none showed.

Eventually another good sister came out and rang the bell and we all returned to our classrooms.

On that hot June day, we lost our fear, and respect, for corporal punishment.

Chapter 2 -Nov. 22, 1992

THE WOODS CAN
MAKE YOU HUMBLE

THE POSITION I hold at this newspaper can quickly teach you humility.

To set the record straight, I am not a golfer. I've found myself playing golf in recent years because my frequent tennis partner, Dr. Tom Stringer of Inverness, wanted to play something in which he could beat me.

On one of my first visits to a golf course, there was a foursome in front of us with whom I was acquainted. They were intrigued to see me on a golf course and one of the players yelled back, "Gerry, we didn't even know you played."

I solved the riddle for them quickly by lining my tee shot through the window of one of the golf course maintenance trucks that was actually sitting in back of the tee.

Trust me, that was a difficult shot.

My game has improved some, but my partners still always know to stand behind me.

It was with some apprehension that I agreed recently to play at the opening of the new Black Diamond course in Lecanto. I've been a guest at the old Black Diamond course and it is magnificent. Tom Fazio, the world's top golf course designer, prepared the old course and had worked with owner Stan Olsen to design the new nine-hole course.

But playing the old course with friends like Steve Lamb is not that intimidating. When Lamb and I play together, it's like a contest to see who can hit the most balls into the canyon. The only competition is to see who runs out of balls first.

I was especially lured by the fact that Tom Fazio was going to be playing on the first official day of golf at the new course. So I decided that even though I'm a horrible golfer, I couldn't pass up the chance to see the new course with about 40 other players invited by Stan Olsen.

Playing with good golfers would be different, but I thought I could just fade into the pack and enjoy the morning.

Apprehension began to grow when I showed up at Black Diamond that Wednesday morning and several county commissioners quickly informed me that they had too much pride to play. "Are you kidding," county commission chairman Gary Bartell said. "These guys would die laughing if they saw me play. I'm just here for the ribbon cutting."

As the crowd gathered to watch the ribbon-cutting ceremony at the course, one of the Chronicle's sports writers approached me and said, "I didn't even know you played golf."

"I really don't," I replied.

"Well why are you teamed up with Fazio and Olsen?" he queried.

Sure enough, two of my partners were Olsen and Fazio. I thought back to the last weekend I played golf and I didn't hit a single tee-shot clean. Yet here I was on the first tee of a beautiful new golf course with the owner and the world-famous designer.

I sensed I was in for a long morning. All I could see was the opportunity to hit repeated slices into the woods. The easiest way to hit a slice is to think you're going to hit a slice.

We approached the tee and introductions were made. Fazio was telling the others about his previous day on a Palm Springs golf course with Nick Faldo.

I began to get nervous. I never get nervous, but here I was about to make a fool of myself in front of the top golf course designer in the world. Well, I thought, maybe he just designs golf courses and doesn't play that well.

Fazio stepped up to the tee and cleanly hit his drive 275 yards into the middle of the fairway. So much for not being able to play golf.

It was my turn. I could see the slice. There were no maintenance trucks around so I couldn't knock out any more windows.

I stepped up to the ball, thought about my slice, and then hit the ball 175 yards right down the middle of the fairway. I didn't care about what else happened during the day, at least I didn't lose face on the first hole.

I triumphantly turned and found Fazio standing at my side.

Fazio looked out at my ball and calmly said, "Don't feel so bad, Gerry. Go ahead and hit another ball."

I was devastated. "Tom, you don't understand. That's as good as it gets."

He quickly came to understand. That turned out to be my best shot of the day.

It turned out to be a delightful experience and it was a great way to see Citrus County's most exclusive community. Black Diamond truly is a diamond of a development.

Fazio was gracious, even when he had to search for my ball in the woods on the fourth hole. I bet Nick Faldo can't say that he had Tom Fazio looking for his ball in the woods.

Chapter 3 - Nov. 17, 1996

———— ∾∾ ————

THERE ARE TIMES TO
APPRECIATE YOUR AGE

IF WE GET seven lives before our time is up, I used two of them over the last week.

I started the week by joining my children for a day of surfing in the Atlantic Ocean. They are teenagers and much better equipped for the sport. But I refuse to admit the birthdays have built up and still visit the ocean on occasion.

While sitting on our surfboards about a quarter-mile off shore enjoying the waves, my teenage son asked, "Dad, did you see that shark?"

I glared.

Jeremiah is 15 and spends a good part of his life trying to make me feel old.

"Jeremiah, don't say those things," I barked back.

"But, Dad, there really was a shark," he replied nonchalantly. "But there's nothing to worry about. I saw one of those shows on Discovery that said sharks won't hurt you."

I then went into one of those fatherly sermons about the boy who screamed wolf and all the trouble he got into. With enthusiasm, I explained how the wolf eventually ate the boy.

Jeremiah's reply was swift and predictable. "There's another shark right behind you, Dad."

"If you keep this up," I said, "I'm going to leave you out here alone."

He gave me one of those snarls that only a teenager can master and then paddled away.

A short time later, the three of us paddled to shore and as we walked the final twenty feet to the sand, a very distinguishable shark with a mighty fin swam right between the two of us.

"There goes a wolf," said Jeremiah, "but let's make believe we didn't see him. That way we'll really be safe."

• Last Saturday we tried to be cautious and not go out in the rain and wind. The nasty weather had ripped through Pinellas and Pasco counties causing much damage.

But later in the afternoon, the rain seemed to have stopped and things looked calm. The kids wanted to go to the mall in Crystal River, so off we went.

As we drove across State Road 44 and hit Lecanto, I realized we had made a bad decision. A dark black mass of clouds came swirling over the highway.

Right as we crossed County Road 491, I saw what I didn't want to see. The clouds to the south suddenly turned a blue-green.

I'd been through a few tornadoes in Florida and that blue-green was a color you never forget.

"Why don't we pull into the convenience store," my wife Janet said as we crossed the road.

Indecision got the best of me.

"The Chronicle office is right up the road. We can make it there," I replied.

We didn't.

Just as we came over the hill and passed Cowboy Junction, we knew that our choices were limited. Three hundred yards to the southwest was a very clear tornado rumbling across the pasture.

It was coming right at us.

It's funny in a way when you face the fury of Mother Nature. You don't have time to be afraid. Fatalism takes over. What's going to happen is going to happen.

Unless of course I can get out of the way.

I mashed the car into reverse and started going backwards on S.R. 44. That probably wasn't the brightest thing to do – if someone was driving behind me, I would have hit them pretty hard.

But we weren't worried about cars at this point. We were worried about that twisting wind with all those cinder blocks inside of it.

Was it just a coincidence that there weren't any other cars around? Probably not. I was most likely the only one dim-witted enough to drive to the mall during a tornado alert.

I quickly realized we weren't going to outrace the tornado going backwards down S.R. 44. I pulled the car into a dirt drive that was covered with trees and yelled for the kids to put their heads down.

The whole area was shaking and I did one of those unexplainable things people who work for newspapers do when they find themselves in the middle of tornadoes. I opened the door to the car to see if I could stand up and take a picture.

The kids and Janet screamed. I closed the door.

Someone said something about "Toto," but mostly the trio of children recited prayers in earnest.

The car shook, the trees snapped and then it was gone.

There was plenty of damage, but fortunately no one in Citrus County was hurt by the tornado.

This weekend I'm going to stay home, paint the walls and appreciate my age.

Chapter 4 - July 1, 2001

 —∞—

BIBLICAL BATTLE ENDS BETTER

THERE WAS A famous time in the Bible when a man, a woman and a snake got together. There was an apple involved in that story, and we've been searching for salvation ever since.

It's a combination we've been fearful of for many years.

I was walking through the house the other day, and as I passed the kitchen, I noticed a snake coiled in the middle of the tiled floor.

It wasn't a huge snake.

But it was a snake.

Now, most honest men in America will admit that they routinely walk past things in the house that need attention. Throughout the years, the male species has developed the ability to avoid paying attention to the obvious.

The kids leave cups on the counter, and we don't put them in the dishwasher. Deep down in the pitted crevices of our chauvinistic brains, we know that our wives will put away the dirty dishes. We are truly liberated men who respect women for their intelligence, good looks and common sense.

But we still know that wives will put the dirty cups into the dishwasher.

Now you may scoff at this deeply developed male trait of avoiding the obvious, but it's the same skill we use when forced to sit outside the dressing room in the department store while wives try on 14 different dresses for some upcoming social event.

We can make ourselves temporarily comatose when the occasion arises.

It's a guy thing.

You can't have one without the other.

But when you have a snake on the floor of the kitchen, even a husband who has a Ph.D. in avoidance must take some action. When you meet a snake in the backyard, the easy response is to shoo it away.

But when a snake makes it into the living quarters, shooing it away doesn't have the same appeal.

Combine this with the fact that daughter Erin has an unnatural fear of all snakes and some sort of immediate capture of the slithering invader made sense. Erin gets married next month and all the plans for the wedding have been completed. It would be a shame if she went comatose based on an indoor snake confrontation and we had to alter the wedding plans.

I decided to go on the attack against the snake. I retrieved a broom and a box and tried to coax the snake into surrender. His response was to spring from his coiled position and lunge at my ankle. I retreated to the family room to regroup. Our cats sat down next to me and for the first time in their feline lives looked at me with the hope that I had an answer to the invader.

These are spoiled cats. They were obviously concerned that they might have to share their food with the snake if I didn't get rid of him. (Snakes are always of the male gender because of what Jim Bob did to Peggy Sue in 1956, but that's another column.)

I went back for a second assault on the snake and he did a particularly snaky thing. He slithered into the cabinet under the kitchen sink and disappeared.

I pulled everything out of the cabinet, but the snake was gone. There was a gap in the cabinet where the pipes came up to the kitchen sink. My adversary had made his escape.

I can't say I was displeased. Capturing a snake in an open box was probably not the smartest thing to try, especially when the snake had already proven its ability to try and nip at my leg.

Several years ago I had a similar confrontation with an alligator that had wandered onto our property and took a position outside of the dog pen. The gator thought our Golden Retriever would make a great lunch. I ran from the kitchen with the same broom and whacked the alligator on the head.

The gator turned and looked at me with his steely eyes and thought: "Buddy, you're an idiot. I'm an alligator, and you're a guy with a broom and I'll chew on you as quickly as I'll chew on your dog."

The gator lunged at me and I ran back to the house. The gator then got up on all four legs and ran away. And I'm not kidding; the gator ran as fast as any dog I've ever seen.

I should have gotten rid of the broom then. The next morning I returned to the kitchen and my friend the snake had retaken his position in the middle of the floor. I got the room, the box and some pool equipment and then made my best decision.

I yelled for my wife.

Together we cornered the snake and got him in the box with a pool skimming net on top. The angry snake coiled and snipped, but to no avail.

Man and woman had come together to conquer the evil snake. Erin was protected, the wedding will go on and life will be good again.

After depositing the snake outdoors, we returned to the kitchen to celebrate our victory with some apple pancakes. As we prepared to eat the apples, there was a bolt of thunder in the distance.

Making the second good decision that morning, I scraped the apples off the pancakes.

No sense in testing fate.

Chapter 5 - May 12, 2002

MOTHERS HOLD IT ALL TOGETHER

THE FIRST TIME my mother ever saw her future husband – my father – he was knocking out the window of a car in the Irish section of the Bronx.

I don't think it was love at first sight.

My father, who was just a teenager at the time, was actually knocking the window out of his own car because he had locked the keys inside and he was late for work.

Thirty years later I repeated the scenario as I raced to be on time at the A&P supermarket in Commack. When my own oldest son was 18, I noticed the side window was knocked out of his truck. I didn't ask what happened. I knew it was the genetic flaw reasserting itself with the latest generation.

I'm sure some future Mulligan is going to knock the window out of his spaceship because he can't find the keys.

My parents ended up being very traditional for their time. My mother stayed home while my father worked. She took the lead as they raised seven children. She didn't get a paycheck, but she earned a living the hard way.

Where I grew up, seven children was the norm. Irish Catholics were very good at making babies.

This past week my mother traveled to Florida to surprise my older brother who was celebrating his 50th birthday. We had a little celebration in Inverness at Stumpknocker'srestaurant. My mother disguised herself as a waitress and tried to take his drink order. It was a nice surprise.

A lot of adults today take for granted that they had great parents who played such a significant role in their lives. Here's my own mother traveling more than 1,000 miles to attend a birthday party. The role never ends. For the good parents, nurturing never stops.

Contrast that with the story about the little Miami girl that is rocking Florida this week.

Rilya Wilson was only 5 years old when the Florida Department of Children and Families lost her. It took more than a year before anyone – including her family – realized she was missing.

It's a crime that young Rilya was lost, but it's a bigger crime that our society has degenerated to the point where so many children are lost.

Over the last three decades, the family structure has deteriorated to the point where the traditional family of the 1960s is no longer the norm. It's now unusual when you have a mother, father and natural children all living in the same household.

Stay-at-home moms are as rare as a Devil Ray's victory.

Somehow the role of the family has changed dramatically and it's doubtful that we can comprehend the significance that will have in the decades to come. We have forgotten that parenting is the most important role that people play in life.

Parents out of control with their own lives are incapable of raising healthy, happy and productive children. Too many parents are turning the upbringing of their children over to the schools or the state.

Is anyone surprised that government can't do a good job of raising children?

Mothers and fathers raise children. I'm pretty darn lucky that my own mother is out there nurturing and reinforcing her children 50 years after the first one was born. Talk about staying power.

Little Rilya Wilson wasn't so lucky. So many other kids are in the same precarious position.

The rest of us should remember to thank our own mothers today. Most have done some pretty remarkable work.

Chapter 6 - June 23, 2002

FATHER'S DAY ON THE LEDGE

IT WAS FATHER'S Day, and my daughter had flown in from Boston to spend the weekend with me.

My job was to find a hotel along the Atlantic Coast so father and daughter could spend the long weekend bonding and running up charges on my credit card. Being in the newspaper business, I'm trained to operate under the pressure of deadlines. That's a nice way to say that I didn't have any hotel reservations when I traveled to the Atlantic Ocean, and was kind of depending on my good looks and great fortune that things would work out.

They didn't.

How was I to know that this weekend getaway was not a unique idea, and that all the quality hotels would be filled up with fathers and daughters who knew how to call in advance?

My daughter was flying from Boston and I was only driving from Citrus County, so I figured I had better get the hotel job done or we'd be sleeping in the back of my Jeep behind the garbage dumpster at the Holiday Inn.

That might be good for my credit card, but it would rate pretty low on the bonding scale.

So, after more than a dozen telephone calls, I finally found a hotel that had a vacancy.

There is a reason you can find vacancies at a single hotel on A1A when all the other hotels are completely booked. That reason is best described in detail by the county health department.

The clerk/owner/housekeeper/maintenance expert/baggage handler greeted me upon my arrival and assured me the reason the pool was locked up shouldn't alarm me. It was locked up, she said, because the health department was still trying to determine the extent of the environmental hazard that existed.

Hey, who needs a pool when you have the Atlantic Ocean?

The room I got was a second-floor oceanfront with a 1960s motif and an outstanding view. What could go wrong?

That question was answered about 10 minutes later.

The toilet was the first thing to object to human occupancy of my oceanfront villa. The flushing mechanism had the accuracy of a Broward County voting booth lever in the 2000 presidential election. It swung freely but didn't get the job done.

I grabbed the key and made a dash down to the front office to see if I could get some help.

The clerk/owner/housekeeper/maintenance expert/baggage handler was just leaving the office and she told me she didn't fix toilets, but she had a good idea. She offered me access to an adjacent empty room so I could utilize those bathroom facilities until ours could be fixed.

I still wasn't giving it much thought that I was the only occupant of the motel.

Being a really flexible person, that sounded like a good compromise to me.

I now had a suite of rooms and at least one working toilet. What more could you want?

I left my oceanfront villa to use the restroom at my second room and take a quick shower in anticipation of my daughter's arrival. Once showered, I left my second room and returned to the first.

With my towel wrapped around the important body parts, I tried to gain entry into my toilet-less quarters.

The heavy salt air has an interesting impact on door locks – especially if the locks haven't been maintained since the Kennedy administration. The lock had the consistency of ground-up Tums, and proceeded to suck my room key into its deteriorating mechanism.

I couldn't get the key out, and it wouldn't turn.

My choices were limited. Since all of my clothes were in the locked room, I had to gain entry. I could have smashed in the front window, but that seemed extreme. Instead, I looked into the room and noticed the kitchen window was open just a crack. There was a six-inch ledge that worked its way around the second story unit, and my destiny became clear.

I wrapped the towel tightly and began to edge along the ledge. Large pointy bushes were below and they would cushion any unfortunate fall. Those same bushes had pointy branches that might also permanently wound me.

Falling was not an option.

I edged all the way around the backside of the building and pulled the screen off the window. While the ocean air had deteriorated the window frame, I was able to push it open.

As I prepared to climb into the room, I wrapped the towel one more time.

"Daddy, what's that man doing," a young voice said from behind me.

I looked down and there was a nice family of four walking up a public beach access trail. Standing there with chairs, umbrellas and open mouths, they were all looking up as I prepared to lift myself through the open window.

"I'm not sure, son," the dad said. "But I think we should call the police."

I tried to assure them there was a good explanation, but I'm not sure I even believed myself. I did get into my room, and I was able to later explain to the police that I was supposed to be there.

They asked me to keep my clothes on and stay off the ledge. I promised I would try.

The next day, the toilets in my second room broke.

I didn't bother to ask for a third room.

Chapter 7 - Jan. 5, 2003

———✦———

A TRULY UNIQUE
CHRISTMAS PRESENT

I GOT AN island for Christmas. Now before you go off thinking that I have a really great wife who purchased me a small Caribbean island with palm trees and rolling surf, let me set the record straight.

My wife (who really is great) didn't buy me the island.

And I certainly didn't buy the thing for myself.

Truth is, the darn thing just showed up.

We live on the big lake in Hernando. And just like every other lake-front resident on the East Side of Citrus County, we've been delighted with the rising water levels of recent months.

We had hacked a trail through the marshy shorefront so we could canoe around the lake. Before Christmas there was only a cranky eight-foot alligator that stood in the way of open waterfront and our dock.

But that's all changed.

On Christmas morning, a 150-foot-long island showed up at our back door.

It wasn't gift-wrapped.

It wasn't filled with palm trees.

And it certainly wasn't moving.

It just blew in.

It seems that the gusty pre-Christmas weather we experienced in Citrus County did a job on the huge island that sits in the middle of the Hernando lake.

For years, the island has been the home to thousands of migrating birds that use the tangled mess as the perfect breeding ground.

We call it Bird Island. (But we also call Steve Spurrier the Gator coach, so take that for what it's worth.)

The 35-mile-per-hour winds of Christmas Eve apparently tore free a 150-foot portion of Bird Island and sent it straight across the lake to my back yard.

The island managed to plug itself into my canoe trail.

We can't get the canoe out, and the new kayaks we purchased for Christmas are land-locked.

Even the cranky eight-foot alligator is bewildered. Each day he crawls out of the muck, takes one look at the new landscape and goes back below.

I thought about officially annexing the island as part of my back yard, but I'm sure that Property Appraiser Ron Schultz would immediately hike my property assessment and figure out a way to tax me.

Using his infamous Sugarmill Woods cow theory, I'm sure the island is worth more than a million dollars.

So here's my thought. We're going to have an auction for Mulligan's Island. While the value may be about $1 million for this weed-infested tangle of birds and beasts, I won't accept anything more than $50,000.

This is a deal.

I will take sealed bids at my Meadowcrest office until noon on Wednesday. Cashier checks will be appreciated. The one caveat is that the winning bidder must come to my backyard and remove their new island.

You can haul it off anywhere you'd like, just get it out of our canoe trail!

To seal the deal, I'll throw in one cranky alligator. And I'll even try to soften up the property appraiser for the winner.

Naming rights are included with the purchase.

Chapter 8 - Jan. 19, 2003

SHORT LIFE EXPIRES FOR MULLIGAN'S ISLAND

THERE WAS A lot of interest in my island.

As I noted a few weeks back, I got an island for Christmas. It blew up in my back yard on Lake Hernando. A 150-foot island of twigs, bushes and birds suddenly blocked in our once wide open lakefront.

I expressed fear that property appraiser Ron Schultz was going to figure out a way to levy a tax against me over my newfound floating island. I offered to auction off the island and got plenty of response.

Some offered to buy the island. One reader wanted to homestead it. Another suggested we take up occupancy and declare our independence from Citrus County.

County Commissioner Josh Wooten had one of the most interesting suggestions.

Wooten, who represents the Hernando area, proposed that he could get with Realtor Kevin Cunningham and sell the island to a developer. Blake Longacre's name came up.

Wooten suggested that condominiums could be constructed on

my island and if the neighbors objected, the island could simply be hauled off to another locale.

If we kept moving the condos, Wooten suggested, we'd eventually find an acceptable home.

It's nice to see that government can be so flexible.

My fears about tax liability have been realized. The following is the e-mail I received from Property Appraiser Ron Schultz.

"You have indicated that a portion of Bird Island has migrated to your back yard. If a portion has accreted to the uplands, I assure you that we will tax it appropriately.

"Assuming that you wish to minimize the tax liability on your nest egg, then I assume that you will be applying for a classified-use agricultural assessment.

"My staff assures me that Bird Island is not up to holding cattle, and that your plan to ranch this portion will not float. Under the circumstances, I suggest that you discuss with the alligator her plans for her progeny. Working closely together, you may be able to raise enough alligators to qualify as a commercial agricultural activity."

Schultz went on to say, "Based on recent articles in the Chronicle, I understand that property that does not land into any other category is zoned MXU. Given that you own a lot on Kings Bay, I suggest that you consider towing your Christmas gift there, allow it to accrete to that parcel where you could open a timeshare, eco-tourism campground. If you can convince the alligator to remain with you, that will assure a rapid turnover in tenants."

He's a very helpful public servant, wouldn't you agree?

Not to be outdone, Melanie Hensley, the Chief Deputy of the Citrus County Property Appraiser's Office had to step in and be heard. We "want to tour the island to be sure we assess every square inch (forget that square-foot assessment we normally use). We aren't interested in assessing the alligator unless, of course, you are intending to start an alligator farm, in which case there will also be Tangible Personal Property taxes to be assessed. If you are keeping the birds and decide to buy cages for them ... again, Tangible Personal Property Taxes."

Being the ever-vigilant public servant, Mrs. Hensley pointed out, "I was wondering if you had checked with DEP and the Army Corps of Engineers before hacking a trail through the marshy shorefront.

"They, of course, will want their fair share in the say of whether or not this was legal and, of course, there are permits for hacking and fees to be paid, too."

Mrs. Hensley has great potential to be almost as helpful as Mr. Schultz was.

I hate to disappoint the tax-man (and woman), but the good news is that Mulligan's Island is gone.

Before I could put it on Ebay, the county took action.

On Wednesday of last week, the county's aquatic services department showed up in Hernando Lake. They dispatched two huge machines that gobbled up much of the floating debris that littered the lake. Their efficiency was amazing.

My 150-foot-long island was the largest victim.

Our canoe once again has access to the great waters of Hernando Lake.

No island, no condos, no taxes.

Life is good again.

Chapter 9 - Aug. 15, 2004

───────◆◆◆───────

WE'RE TOO NEW TO BE EVACUATED

I DON'T WANT to be a whiner. I don't even like whiners.

But after living in our new house in Crystal River for just one month, we were ordered out. We'd just moved to town and already they were telling us to leave.

I felt like whining.

As Hurricane Charley began its ramble through the Florida Keys and up the coastline of the Sunshine State on Friday, local officials made the call that everyone who lived along our coastline had to get out.

It was a smart call to make at the time. The threat of a 10-foot storm surge slashing through our coastline was reminiscent of the March 13 "no-name" storm back in 1993.

For a novice evacuee, I didn't know what to take.

My toothbrush; a change of clothes; sneakers and a good book all seemed logical for our retreat from the coastline. Two days before the evacuation order, we had a new 50-inch television delivered to the house.

I got out the tape measure to see if I could get the television into the back of the Jeep.

"You can't take the television," my wife and fellow evacuee told me.

"I haven't seen the Mets play a single game on this thing yet," I said. "The television is coming. I'm putting my foot down."

The television did not make the trip.

The dog made the trip, but the cat did not. Our cat doesn't like traveling. Whenever he's placed in the car for a ride to the veterinarian, he produces a high-pitched meow at the rate of 45 per minute. I would rather strap myself to the city dock and take the full force of the hurricane than ride in a car for 25 miles with the cat.

I traded the cat for the big-screen television. The way I figured it, if Hurricane Charley washed the house and my big-screen television away – it wouldn't be a total loss if the cat went with them.

I'm kidding; I really like cats, but this feline has severe personality issues. Just last week, I came home from a long day at the office listening to politicians. The cat welcomed me at the garage door. He looked me straight in the eye and did his business on the floor right in front of me.

The cat is like a teenager who has just been told he can't take the family car to the prom.

As we evacuated, we took soft drinks, peanuts and crackers, thus covering all major food groups. We took pillows, blankets and playing cards.

And for good luck, we took a golf club.

During the 1993 storm, my golf clubs were at a friend's house in Crystal River. I think I had left them in the trunk of Steve Lamb's car. After the storm came, Steve called me up and confessed that all of his furnishings got washed away, including my golf clubs.

I wasn't upset, because I'm really lousy at golf. About two months after the storm, we had a call from someone at the Plantation Inn who found the clubs where they had been washed away into a ditch. They were pretty rusted, but I took them back home.

By taking my driver with me, I made sure that 2004 would not be a repeat of 1993.

The cat appreciated the symbolism.

Chapter 10 - 2004

Redefining a good weekend

I BELIEVE OUR neighbors are putting a petition together to ask us to move out of Crystal River.

It is not that I'm taking this personally, but we moved into a new house on the river about 10 weeks ago. In those 10 weeks, we've had four hurricanes, three separate flooding events and four forced evacuations by county emergency personnel.

We've had three occasions where the electricity has gone off for extended periods, twice where flood waters have gotten into the garage and three times where flood waters have crossed the streets.

It's also been noted by the neighbors that our dog has a shrill bark.

I personally refuse to take responsibility for the horrendous weather that has beset us in recent weeks, but I'm not sure the neighbors are buying it.

I had one miraculous moment during the last week. When I got out of bed on Monday morning, I forgot we didn't have any power. I walked into the kitchen for my morning ritual of making a hot cup of tea. I filled the kettle with water and went to turn on the electric stove and then remembered our powerless dilemma.

At that very moment the power flickered on.

The water boiled and I poured my cup of tea. At the exact moment I put the kettle back on the stove, the power again blinked off.

Sometimes you just live right.

Along with thousands of other Citrus County residents, we've redefined what a good weekend looks like. Our expectations have been lowered.

It's a good weekend now when the winds don't blow over 65 mph.

It's a good weekend when you don't have to look at the Weather Channel once.

It's a good weekend when you don't have to spend hours figuring out how to get everything you own up off the garage floor.

It's a good weekend when you decide to use the barbecue grill in the back yard because it's an option, not the only way you can cook something.

It's a good weekend when you don't sit around worrying that the rest of the roof at Pete's Pier is going to blow off and come crashing through your living room window.

It's a good weekend when you have a candlelight dinner with your wife because it's romantic and not because you're trying to save the batteries in the flashlight.

It's a good weekend when you can take the dog for a walk so he can do his business and not get that look, "Hey buddy, I might be a dog, but I'm still not going outside."

It's a good weekend when your ability to look into the night's sky is because a contractor put a skylight in your bedroom, instead of an oak tree making an uninvited entry into your home.

It's a good weekend when your kayak is a form of recreation, not transportation.

It's a good weekend when your water and ice comes across a tiki bar with a little bit of scotch, as opposed to getting your water and ice out of the back end of a Salvation Army relief truck.

It's a good weekend when the only Hurricanes around that are kicking up a fuss are the members of the Citrus High School football team.

I hope you have a good weekend.

Chapter 11 - April 10, 2005

───※───

MINI-VAN WRAP AND A GAP

A MALE COWORKER complained the other day that he could never get a direct answer from his loving wife. "It's like we speak different languages," he said.

While husbands and wives have had trouble communicating for as long as there have been husbands and wives, I recently learned that there is also a communication gap between the generations.

We had the misfortune to recently need the emergency room at Citrus Memorial Hospital. My mother-in-law broke her kneecap after trying to high-vault over a gate. Joan Hemsworth, who lives at the Inverness Golf and Country Club, is in better shape than most women 50 years her junior. But she promises to give up the high jump.

The kneecap needed surgery and my wife, her dad, Ed Hemsworth, and myself, all found ourselves at the hospital late on a wet and windy March evening. Once the surgery was complete and Joan went to sleep, we all decided it was time to go home.

I offered to go out into the rainy evening and retrieve Ed's car from the parking lot.

"Remind me, what does the car look like?" I asked.

"It's a mini-van," he said.

"How can I tell it from the thousand other mini-vans out there?" I asked.

He thought for a minute and then said: "It has an American flag on the antenna."

OK, a mini-van with an American flag. I should be able to find that.

So out I went into the parking lots of Citrus Memorial Hospital. Now if you are at all familiar with Citrus Memorial, you know it has grown so much in recent years that the parking lots are spread out all over the place. It's pretty important that you remember exactly where you parked.

Ed had not done that.

Have I mentioned that of those people needing hospital care, the mini-van is the No. 1 vehicle of choice? And have you noticed that every mini-van has an American flag on the antenna?

The first mini-van I found with an American flag on the antenna was light blue. I tried the key and it didn't work.

My feet were soaking wet by the time I found the second mini-van with an American flag.

"Hey buddy, what are you doing," a man asked as he walked through the rainstorm. "You trying to steal my car?"

"Sorry, I'm looking for a mini-van," I replied.

"Well, stay away from mine," he barked.

So with a bit more trepidation, I spent the next 15 minutes walking around in the torrential rain looking for the Hemsworth mini-van. Since visiting hours had passed, most of the vehicles were pulling out of the parking lot.

I was wet, cranky and beginning to lose confidence that I was going to find the car in question. After a while, only one mini-van remained in the parking lot.

This mini-van was some type of strange model, because it was completely covered in what appeared to be Saran Wrap. From top to bottom, the car was wrapped up like a Christmas present in clear plastic.

Just like all the other mini-vans, it also had a very small American flag on the antenna.

I was soaking wet and was willing to try anything. I went over to the Saran-wrapped mini-van and tried the key.

It worked.

I shook off as much water as I could and climbed into the one-of-a-kind vehicle.

When I drove back to the hospital to pick up Ed, I asked him why he hadn't mentioned that all that I had to look for was the Saran-wrapped mini-van.

Ed explained the wrapping was necessary because earlier in the day he had left the tail-gate open in the high position and tried to back the van into the garage. The van bent, the house didn't.

Since it was raining, Ed's immediate answer was to give the car a good wrapping with plastic.

"But Ed," I asked. "Why did you not tell me?"

"I thought the flag would have been enough," he said.

When guys can't give each other directions, you know the world is really in trouble.

Chapter 12 - Oct. 30, 2005

OH, THE JOYS OF BOAT OWNERSHIP

I HAVE BEEN unceremoniously welcomed into the family of Citrus County boat owners.

And yes, my wallet is open.

As luck would have it, we purchased a pontoon boat a week before I did something incredibly stupid. While surfing in some hurricane waves on the Atlantic coast, I had an accident and a fin went through my right hand. It took 11 hours in an emergency room, one hour in surgery and a whole bunch of stitches to put my right hand back together.

And yes, I'm right handed.

So when we went to pick up our pontoon boat, I wasn't going to be the one doing the heavy lifting. I drafted our two sons, Jeremiah and Jeff, to come to my assistance in picking up the boat, transporting it to Pete's Pier in Crystal River, and then motoring it over to our dock.

Both Jeremiah and Jeff are experienced with boats and fully capable of handling any situation that comes up.

Almost.

The boys backed the boat down the ramp and smoothly launched.

That was a good sign.

They started the engine up and it purred like on the commercials.

That was a good sign.

They waved goodbye and took off. The boat suddenly lurched, the engine jumped up and then all mechanical activity stopped. The boys both stumbled along the deck and came close to falling into the water.

That was a bad sign.

So there I was. An official boat owner for about 1 minute and 32 seconds and trouble had already arrived.

My seaworthy sons stumbled around the deck looking for the problem. Apparently they failed to secure the lines and one had gotten wrapped in the prop.

One of the great things about being a boat owner is that you get to have these stress-producing experiences at public boat ramps while a dozen people stand around and gawk at you. They poke each other in the ribs, laugh and point.

It's great fun.

Your job as the boat owner is to then act like this is an everyday experience and you're not fazed by the absurd fact that you are drifting out to sea with a boat that is no longer responding.

My sons performed well.

As they drifted away, a cracker fisherman sitting on his boat whittling a piece of driftwood said to them: "Would you like me to call 911."

Then he laughed.

My polite son said: "No thank you, sir."

The same son later admitted he would have killed the cracker fisherman if he could have gotten just a little bit closer to him.

But they didn't get closer because they were too busy drifting out to sea with the now-disabled boat. I was still on land and had owned the boat for about 5 minutes and 46 seconds and was wondering when the fun was going to begin.

Jeff is a fireman and he is trained to take immediate action when emergency situations arise. He decided to jump off the boat.

I had only owned the boat for about 7 minutes and people were already abandoning ship.

A larger crowd was gathering on the docks at Pete's Pier because this is obviously the most fun you have as a boat owner. Watching other people self-destruct is quite a spectator sport in Crystal River.

Jeff had freed the line from the prop but the engine and battery were now not responding. Using his best fireman initiative, Jeff put the line in his teeth and began to swim. He pulled the boat toward the main dock.

Ten minutes, 37 seconds of boat ownership and already I had a disabled vessel and Humphrey Bogart in the water doing a rescue.

It was at that point that I saw the fish. Jeff is 6-foot-2 and weighs in at about 200 pounds.

The fish was bigger.

I don't know if you still call them fish when they grow to be over 200 pounds – sea creature seems like a more appropriate term.

So as Jeff swam pulling the boat, the 200-pound sea creature simply circled behind him trying to figure out if he could swallow a swimmer that big.

Now, after about 15 minutes of boat ownership I was envisioning the headline in the next day's paper: "Son's rescue goes bad; 200-pound tarpon devours swimmer."

Jeff was oblivious to his swimming partner and I didn't think it made good sense to bring it to his attention until he got out of the water.

He survived and the visiting tarpon went back under the dock to wait for a smaller appetizer.

So after 21 minutes, 47 seconds of boat ownership, I had a disabled vessel, got our first official tow, had a man overboard, almost witnessed the murder of a cracker fisherman, watched a 200-pound sea creature consider eating my son and got directions to West Marine, where I had to spend lots of money to get the boat working again. It should be noted that I hadn't even been on the boat yet!

When does the fun begin?

Chapter 13 - Sept. 25, 2005

—◦◦◦—

DUCT TAPE AND FAMILY VALUES

I RECENTLY DISCOVERED that a single room in my family's home shaped my life.

It was the bathroom.

It wasn't any bathroom – it was the single full bathroom in our home, and it served the needs of seven children and two adults for many years.

It was a very valuable room. And just like the confessional at St. Patrick's Cathedral after the Yankees lost two out of three to the Red Sox, it was almost never empty.

This past weekend, my brother and I visited the family home where our parents still reside and share that same bathroom.

After 43 years, not much has changed.

The bathroom is on the second floor of the homestead. Directly below the second-floor bathroom is the kitchen, and directly below where the family's single shower sits is the family's kitchen table.

There is a relationship.

It's not clear when you're a kid, but the peculiar habits of your parents somehow seep into the genes of your very existence.

You don't want it to happen, but it does.

Since about the mid-1960s, our family's single shower just has not been right. At certain moments directly tied to the long showers that one of my many sisters would take, the ceiling above the kitchen table would fill with water. It was our custom for the entire family to gather around the kitchen table for the evening meal. The meat loaf would be sliced, the canned green beans heated and the mashed potatoes served.

At the moment we would finish the family prayer, the ceiling would come crashing down on the kitchen table.

Water would splash and children would dive for cover.

My mother's hands would cover her face in horror and my father would curse the plumbers of the world.

But here's the rub: There was never a plumber. Never was, never would be.

My father was an engineer with NASA and in his mind there is not a house fix-it project that he couldn't handle.

On that first evening in the 1960s when the roof came crashing onto our kitchen table, my father gathered the tools of the trade and went to work. He tore out the tile, found the leak and made the appropriate repairs.

He put new plaster on the ceiling and painted it the appropriate white.

He was proud of his accomplishment.

A few months later we were sitting at that same kitchen table when the roof once again came crashing down. The water splashed. The kids dove for cover. The mother covered her face and prayed. The father cursed the plumbers.

For my entire childhood my father worked on that bathroom. The girls kept taking long showers and the water continued to drip through to the bottom floor.

He put in new plumbing, he retiled the floors and walls, he

re-plastered the ceiling and he painted. And then he did it all over again. And again.

At one point my father was close to defeat. Instead of putting new plaster up on the ceiling and painting it white, he put a trap door right above the kitchen table. When the pipes would leak he would simply climb up through the ceiling and look for the offending pipe.

Calling a plumber was never a serious consideration.

So this last week when we visited the family homestead, we were not surprised when one of our sisters gave us a warning. "Don't sit on the toilet in the upstairs bathroom. I'm afraid the floor is about to give way and the whole ceiling is going to come crashing down."

While he is now retired, my father's NASA training has helped him cope with the curse of second-floor plumbing. Instead of replacing the crumbling tiles in the shower, my father has put up a see-through plastic wall covering the shower plumbing. The plastic is fastened with duct tape, which in an Irish family is almost the same thing as having a plumber.

Plastic curtains shield any crack in the wall tiles that could be responsible for the leak. Duct tape protects those areas in question.

After 43 years there is little hope left that the shower's leaking will be stopped. It's only a matter of time before the ceiling comes crashing down during a family dinner.

But still no plumber will be called.

Duct tape. Plastic screening. Trap doors.

Some might look at this as a failure to admit defeat.

But in our family it is a matter of principle.

It's a matter of family pride. We're not going to let four decades of a leaking shower get us down. We're going to find a solution. And we're going to buy more duct tape.

Our family values involve hard work and duct tape. We are Irish-Americans. We are proud. And we are wet.

Chapter 15 - Sept. 2, 2007

JUST ANOTHER STUPID AMERICAN

As a man, I have been blessed with the gene that gives me the ability to drive an automobile better than, well, anyone else on the planet.

Most men have this gene, which is why from the beginning of the automobile age, most men drive the cars. This same gene helps us always be right when we're having a disagreement with our spouses. (This may also be the gene responsible for the high divorce rate in the United States.)

Which brings me to my recent trip to Ireland and the fact that the English – back when they ruled the world – insisted that the Irish also drive on the wrong side of the road. If we had lost the Revolutionary War, we Americans also would now be driving on the wrong side of the road, drinking tea and saluting the Queen Mum instead of Queen Latifah.

When you're forced to drive on the wrong side of the road, the X and Y chromosomes get mixed up and one's ability to be the best driver in the world gets scrambled. Very scrambled.

On my very first evening in Ireland, I managed to do a swift U-turn in the middle of Main Street in Glengarriff. I was proud of my driving maneuver until my right front tire touched the curb and immediately exploded.

In Ireland, they apparently make their curbs out of a limestone that has a sharpened edge. If you just bump it, your tire is rendered useless. The edge sharpening is sponsored by the Irish Tire Manufacturer's Association.

Some very helpful Irish lads were on hand right after my mishap to point their fingers and say "Ha! Another stupid American."

It's a great country where the 12-year-olds drink Guinness with lunch.

On that same day, in the picturesque city of Kenmare, I managed a little fender-bender in a parking lot during a rainstorm. While you drive on the left-hand side of the road in Ireland, their parking lots are just like any Kmart shopping center at Christmas. It's every man for himself.

There was group of boys on bikes nearby and they watched the incident with knowing smirks.

Later that week, I was attempting to be a nice guy and go fetch the car during a rainstorm. Our group was listening to music in one of the pubs and I didn't want to make them get wet going to the car.

So I got in my vehicle and pulled out into the Main Street of the same Glengarriff when a motorist in front of me started to back up. I started to back up to avoid the oncoming vehicle and banged on my horn.

The problem with Irish vehicles is that none of the mirrors are in the right place. Foreign motorists always look above their right shoulders to see what's behind them. In Ireland the rearview mirror is really to your left.

So I saw nothing in my rearview mirror as I backed up in the rainstorm because the rearview mirror wasn't where it was supposed to be. In fact, there was no mirror, so I didn't see the big traffic sign that somehow jumped out and got behind my car.

I banged the pole and managed to break one of the lights. The dent

– in my opinion – was only minor.

As I got out of the car into the rain to inspect the damage, the same Guinness-inspired 12-year-olds miraculously appeared to point and say "Ha! Another stupid American."

"No," I replied, "I'm the same stupid American from yesterday."

The very next day, I took a full carload of relatives on a ride around the Ring of Kerry when we pulled into the picturesque town of Waterville. Daughter Jessica pointed out a restaurant and gave the command to stop.

Did I mention that it was raining?

I immediately pulled into a parking spot, hit the curb and heard a loud bang.

Yet another tire fell victim to the fine work of the Irish Tire Manufacturer's Association curb-sharpening program. And you guessed it, when I got out of the car to examine my handiwork, there was a very similar-looking group of fine Irish lads riding their bikes, pointing at me with glee and saying "Ha! Another stupid American."

I felt like I spent more time on my vacation looking underneath my rental car than I did looking at the beautiful scenery.

When we finally arrived back at Tampa International Airport after a full 24 hours of traveling, we took our little bus to the long-term parking lot. It was midnight when we took the elevator to the top floor of the parking garage and lugged our bags over to my car.

And sure enough, there was my fine American car, with the steering wheel on the side where it belongs.

The only problem was that the car had a flat tire.

I looked behind me expecting to see a group of 12-year-olds on bikes.

But my wife and I were alone. At midnight. In the dark. With a flat tire.

Did I mention it was about to rain?

Chapter 15 - Sept. 27, 2007

RATS OVERBOARD!

WHEN YOU ARE the captain of a boat, there are many privileges that come your way.

You get to make the toasts at all official dinners.

You get the nicest cabin.

And in the best of times, you might be asked to officiate at a wedding of some fire-fighter and his fiancée who decided to elope.

In the worst of times, you are also in charge of all disasters.

They were not the best of times last Saturday morning.

I was the captain of my aging pontoon boat as we chugged out the Crystal River with a group of volunteers who were participating in the annual Save Our Waters Week Adopt-a-Shore cleanup.

We had three kayaks attached to the pontoon so we could gain access to the river shoreline and get at the trash. We had rakes, nets and other tools that would help us get the job done.

As we traveled out the river toward our destination west of the Salt River bridge, Paul Perregaux, a member of the Crystal River Rotary Club and a cleanup volunteer, was telling us a story about growing up in the northeast.

All of a sudden Paul's story concluded with the comment, "Hey, that's a big rat."

As I was driving the boat and dragging three kayaks behind, I wasn't paying absolute attention to every detail of Paul's story and I thought the "rat" in question was just part of the story.

Then Paul said again, "That's a really big rat."

Paul was not reminiscing about his childhood, he was talking about a big rat that climbed out from under his seat and scurried to the front of our 20-foot pontoon boat.

That's about when the screaming started.

All of my boat occupants – excluding the rat – had the same irrational reaction.

Somewhere deep in the human brain, it's been hardwired that if you are trapped on a 20-foot boat with a rat, you should stand up on your seat and scream.

Everyone stood and screamed.

That didn't turn out to be an effective defense.

No. 1, rats are used to screaming. And No. 2, if the rat wanted to jump up on a pontoon boat seat, he could do so pretty easily.

The first lesson I learned as captain of this rat-carrying boat was that you should never abandon the post behind the wheel to go after the rat unless you first put the boat engine into neutral.

I picked up a rake to try and swat the rat and the boat decided it was time to do a right-hand turn and head for the shoreline. Running aground was not going to make it that much more fun to be stuck on a boat with a rat.

I got back behind the wheel.

We all suddenly realized that we had a secret weapon on board this particular pontoon boat. Our two Yorkshire Terriers – Wilson and Duffy – were on board and Yorkies were originally bred as "rat terriers."

Their genes are filled with rat-hunting tendencies. As far as rats are concerned, Yorkies are trained killers.

I looked at the Yorkies and ordered them to "Go get the rat!"

The two Yorkies looked at me and simultaneously had the same reaction. If they could have said, "Get a life," they would have. But since the Yorkies can't speak, they did the next best thing and jumped up on the seat by my wife and got in her lap.

If they could have screamed, they would have.

By this time, the rat had climbed under another boat seat and my helpful crew decided the best thing they could do was abandon ship.

My wife and the Yorkies got into the first kayak and pushed off.

Paul, realizing that nowhere in the Rotary Four-Way-Test is there a line about abandoning ship, volunteered to stay aboard and fight the rat.

Using our rakes and nets, we beat about the boat until the rat realized he was trapped. The rat looked at the crazed boaters with rakes and then at the Gulf of Mexico. He decided he had a better chance in the Gulf of Mexico, so he simply took a running leap off the end of the pontoon and swam away.

It was a very graceful rat dive and to my surprise, the rat never again surfaced. Paul suggested that rats swim underwater, which could produce a whole new set of anxieties along with new rounds of yelling and screaming.

As luck would have it, the next boat over contained one Dr. KC. Nayfield, the Crystal River veterinarian and animal lover extraordinaire.

As we cheered our victory over the rat, Dr. Nayfield pointed out: "I'm going to have to report this to the SPCA. They do have rules about cruelty to rats."

Chapter 16 - May 17, 2009

VALUABLE PRESSURE-
WASHING LESSONS

I PURCHASED MY darling wife a pressure washer for Mother's Day.

Just call me a romantic.

Several years ago I got her a boat anchor for Christmas.

These are gifts she asks for. I am not crazy enough to buy such things if they aren't requested.

It was a pressure washer she wanted, and that's what she got.

Retired two years from the school system, she still has not learned to relax. The pressure washer fit right into her busy workday. She cleaned the back porch thoroughly and then eyed our old pontoon boat sitting at the end of the dock.

The boat was getting pretty moldy and a good pressure wash would brighten things right up. So she hauled the pressure washer to the end of the dock, connected the hose and got to work.

Wherever my wife travels around the house, our two Yorkies go with her to watch for birds or to bark at or other imaginary enemies. So the Yorkies sat at the end of the dock and watched the cleaning frenzy take place.

She used the full power of the pressure washer to get rid of the mold that covered the outside of the boat. It was when she finished the job that she looked around and realized that only one dog remained on the dock watching her.

Wilson, the 6-pound Yorkie, remained in his usual position. But Duffy, his 2-pound half-brother, was nowhere to be seen.

As she was wrapping up the power-wash equipment, she noticed out of the corner of her eye something climbing out of the mud of a Crystal River low tide.

It was the dog.

The 2-pound dog was apparently standing on the dock and must have been hit with a blast from the pressure washer and got knocked out into the river.

Duffy was coughing up water and goop. Janet jumped into the river and rescued the dazed animal and immediately rushed him off to the veterinarian's office.

Now even though I was at work during this entire encounter, there were a few things I learned from the affair.

First, you cannot laugh when your wife calls you at the office and tells you that she just pressure washed the dog into the river – unless, of course, you don't mind sleeping on the couch for the foreseeable future.

The second learning experience is that while it does not seem biologically possible, a 2-pound dog can swallow more than 2 pounds of goop and those 2 pounds of goop can be barfed up on every clean surface of a house in less than 60 minutes.

And the third and final learning experience is that any money you thought you might save by purchasing your wife a gift-wrapped pressure washer is really a dangerous illusion. Those savings will quickly go down the drain when you add up the cost of three trips to the veterinarian's emergency room over a 24-hour period.

The final outcome is what really counts: The boat is clean, the dog has recovered and I am now off the couch.

Chapter 17 - June 2010

Praying that things get better

A FEW YEARS back the bishop from Dublin, Ireland cold called me and asked if I could help him get access to play golf at Black Diamond Ranch.

He was a golf enthusiast and had read about the amazing quarry holes at our world famous course.

With a name like Mulligan he figured he could not go wrong.

And he was right.

I immediately agreed to help out because you never know when you're going to need a little help with the Big Guy upstairs. Bishops often get the unlisted cell number.

He arrived a few weeks later and we played the course together. The bishop was an outstanding golfer and I asked him how he got so good with his busy schedule.

"I find time every day to practice," he told me.

He politely asked how often I practiced and I admitted to him that my game was more dependent on prayer.

"Practice is much better for a consistent game," he advised me.

I proceeded to hit the ball high in the air and together the Bishop and I watched it drop right into water.

We stood in silence until the Bishop said: "Maybe you should pray more often."

I love a bishop with a sense of humor.

The bishop did have some relevant advice for those of us in Citrus County trying to work our way out of the current difficult times.

There are days when it seems that in our county and our country-negative events are overtaking us. Wicked violence, destructive drugs, self indulgence and a collective lack of initiative seems to be eating away at our national momentum.

The bishop had participated for many years in the talks to resolve the differences between Ireland and Northern Ireland. They were suffering with many of the same maladies that seem to be eating away at us, but their violence was much more organized and sanctioned.

The talks resulted in all sorts of actions, new laws and proclamations of progress. But most of that was like my golf ball swing - full of a lot of slice.

The bishop explained that The Troubles in Ireland did not calm down until the country figured out how to get more people employed. When the economy started to get better, the bitter factions lost interest in fighting with each other and instead went to work.

There is a predisposed desire of human beings to provide for themselves and their family.

Most find that it's even more fun that fighting.

If government, politics or greed gets in the way of that happening, discontent becomes the prevailing attitude. And that breeds the use of drugs, crime and violence.

Right here in Citrus County we have too many people out of work or under-employed. While some folks are just trying to scratch out a living, others are doing their best to turn the local economy around and start creating jobs.

Jobs make people happy. We all need a purpose. And we all need to provide for our families.

Our education system needs to provide the skill training necessary for people to work. The business community and local government need to work together to create an environment that fosters job growth.

It's not rocket science. It's human nature.

A vibrant economy helped the Irish stop fighting with each other after 400 years of grief.

Creating rules and regulations that limit businesses is counter-productive. It's like praying that my golf slice will go away.

Jesse Panuccio, the Executive Director of the Florida Department of Economic Opportunity, was in town talking to the chamber on Friday. He reminded business leaders that 70 percent of the businesses in the state have less than five employees.

Citrus County is in a tough position because Duke Energy shut down the Crystal River nuclear power plant and 500 high-paying jobs were slashed.

We are going to get those jobs back – but it's going to be through the creation of hundreds of small businesses that have less than five employees. There might be a few big ones, but most of the growth will be small.

Growing the economy and giving citizens the opportunity to work will greatly reduce the propensity of some to indulge in destructive behaviors.

Working people are more content, they pay taxes and they make the community a better place.

Let's get to work.

Chapter 18 - January 2011

———∿∿———

ANGRY MOB IS LOSING THE WAR AGAINST THE GRASSHOPPERS

WE HAD A grasshopper in Crystal River the other day that was half the size of my dog.

Now I admit I have a small dog, but that's still a big grasshopper.

It's not that we have a single grasshopper as big as my dog; it's that in my neighborhood we have thousands of these six-inch buggers jumping all over the place.

We are fortunate to live on the water so almost every one of my neighbors is sensitive about misusing insecticides. The poison can easily get into the water and accidentally kill the fish.

One day, out of frustration, my wife grabbed a plastic bottle of bug killer and sprayed one of the grasshoppers right in the face. The six-inch grasshopper looked her in the eye, sucked down the poison and then let out what sounded like a small burp.

He stuck around and waited for another drink of bug spray but my wife reverted to the ancient art of grasshopper elimination.

She whacked him on the head with her shoe.

And that's where the real competitive story begins.

Our home is tucked into the end of a street and the five women in the neighborhood do an outstanding job of keeping up the landscaping. There are flowers, bushes and plants all over.

The grasshoppers are apparently a plague from an ex-husband of one of these women because they can eat a healthy plant in a day. The grasshoppers, not the ex-husband.

Anyway, the five neighbors have created their own strategic plan of attack on the grasshoppers. With the pesticides off the table, the strategic attack involves a lot of whacking. They have individual goals of elimination and together they work toward victory.

My wife has refined her attacks by purchasing a pair of rubber gloves and smacking her hands together on the unsuspecting grasshoppers. The gloves actually have spikes built into them for the maximum impact.

It's messy but effective.

Neighbor Marguerite is from Alabama where they have a much more direct approach to problems. She originally used the traditional whacking shoe approach, but the guts of one shot out and got her right in the face, which is about as popular as a tax hike at a tea party.

Marguerite now grabs the grasshoppers in her hands and tears the head off.

Alabama is apparently a pretty tough place.

Neighbor Marcy is from Massachusetts and she is much more refined. Ok, she's somewhat refined.

Anyway, she likes to use the soapy water in a plastic bag technique. As a retired high school language arts department chair, she uses her language skills to convince the grasshoppers to get inside the plastic bag where they slowly drown – somewhat like Gov. Dukakis did after he drove that tank in the parade all those years ago.

Neighbors Ann and Valerie have their own issues. Ann won't kill the grasshoppers, but spends plenty of time pointing out the critters to the other members of the mob.

Valerie was fine with killing her share of grasshoppers until mating season began. She is the head of nursing at one of the large Ocala hospitals and she just can't bring herself to kill the grasshoppers while they are, well, doing it.

She has apparently spent too much time near the hospital maternity ward.

On any given day you can hear one of the neighbors shout: "35."

"I've already gotten 22," another will respond. "And I can't have lunch until I get 50."

Lest you think these ladies are collectively unbalanced, you've got to take a good look at the Lubber grasshopper. The giant, slow moving grasshopper's bright orange, yellow and red colors are a warning that it contains toxins that will make any predator instantly sick.

If a bird eats one of these boys, he'll spend the rest of the day sitting in his nest puking his bird guts out. The family of local raccoons prefers to eat our cat's food.

The state's official grasshopper handbook warns that "If for any reason, you fail to heed the color warning and pick it up; the Lubber grasshopper makes a loud hissing noise and secretes an irritating foul-smelling foamy spray."

Sounds like the perfect house warming gift.

The problem in our neighborhood is that while the ladies will kill hundreds in a given day, the grasshoppers have little to do but sit around, eat plants and then reproduce. Everyday hundreds of new grasshoppers arrive to join the crowd.

Last week we were leaving town for a conference in St. Petersburg. The car was packed and running and I was waiting for my wife to join me. Not being the most patient guy in the world, it took less than five minutes for me to go back into the house to see what the problem was.

But the house was empty. No wife to be found.

I shouted her name and searched all the rooms. As a regular reader of mystery books I immediately imagined the worst. She had been kidnapped and taken away by boat and would be held on a deserted island (or Christmas Island) until I paid the ransom.

So I ran around back looking for evidence of the obvious abduction only to find my wife standing up to her knees in the weeds.

She had her special gloves on. There were dead grasshoppers all around her.

She looked at me sheepishly and said "46."

I'm not sure we are able to proclaim victory yet.

Chapter 19 - April 2011

WATCH OUT WHAT YOU ASK FOR

UNINTENDED CONSEQUENCES RULE the world.

The other day a reader called and asked me for some help. She didn't know where to go to get services for the blind.

I suggested that she use Google Search and look under 'blind services.'

"I'm blind," she told me.

I should have seen that one coming.

It is sometimes difficult to slow down enough and put yourself in another person's situation. It's called empathy and there's a shortage of that going around these days.

I volunteered to do the Google Search myself to find services for the blind in Citrus County. I was chagrined to discover only an agency out of Brooksville provides help locally. I couldn't find much else around.

I passed along the information, but that is not where the story stops. The next day in my private Yahoo email account I had an offer for 'blind services'.

This was not an agency to help the visually impaired, they were offering 10 percent off for new blinds in my house.

I chuckled and thought that was an amazing coincidence. I didn't need new blinds in the house, or at the newspaper, so I deleted the item.

The next day I had two more emails for 'blind services' in my email. The day after that, there were three more offers.

I hate to crowd the 5,000 emails I already have backed up in my Yahoo account so I began to kill and block the emails.

They simply kept coming. Apparently Google and Yahoo got together and decided I am permanently in need of blind services.

There are definitely a few county commissioners who think I am 'blind' to reality, but I don't personally have a need for 'blind services' and I don't need new blinds at the house. (Although those bamboo vertical ones looked really nice).

Apparently it does not matter what I need or want. Currently I reserve a few minutes each day to kill and block 'blind services' email that just keeps coming.

I am just a little concerned because the other day I used Google again to look for some services to help improve by tennis game. I have been slicing the tennis ball lately and I was looking for a tennis pro who could give me lessons on how to 'hit' the ball harder. I asked for references on a tennis 'hit man'.

I'll let you know how that one works out. If the FBI comes around I might need you as a reference.

*On the issue of blind services in Citrus County, there was a time when at least two agencies were providing care and they did not like each other.

That happens sometimes in the non-profit world, agencies who have missions that overlap tend to have tension when dealing with each other.

At the time I was working with Steve Lamb and Wilson Burns to start the United Way in Citrus County. One of the missions of the volunteer board was to try and resolve disagreements between agencies so that we could guarantee donated dollars were being spent efficiently.

So that was the backdrop to how Steve Lamb (of the Crystal Automotive/Motorcycle Group) and myself found ourselves back in the late 1980s sitting in a crowded conference room in Inverness with representatives of the two battling blind services groups. It was a very tense situation and it was obvious the participants had deep misgivings about each other.

Most of the advocates for both blind service's groups were in fact blind and many of them were holding the traditional white cane for the visually impaired. I believe Steve and I were the only two who were not blind at the meeting.

He sat at one end of the long conference table and I sat at the other. That is when, without giving it any prior thought, Steve began the meeting with the perfect opening.

He got everyone's attention and said:

"We obviously do not see eye-to-eye on the issues before us," said Steve.

All the conference participants began to shake and rattle their white canes as I let my head slip and bang on the conference table.

There was much murmuring and a few snickers from the participants, but we actually were able to arrange a cease fire. By the end of the day we all saw things 'eye-to-eye'.

Sort of.

Chapter 20 - July 17, 2011

You know love when you see it

PEOPLE ROUTINELY TELL one another they "love" each other.

In the newspaper business, it's easy to grow cynical at the use of words. Crooks tell us they are innocent, politicians insist they are working for the public good, and everyone proclaims love of country over love of self.

Actions tell us otherwise.

Crooks steal, politicians do what makes them look good and many who proclaim love of country really mean they like being citizens as long as it doesn't become a personal inconvenience.

After 30-plus years in the business, there are some days I don't believe the sun has risen unless I see for myself.

Actions tell the real story. Two quick personal examples:

• I was visiting my son in St. Augustine recently and eventually ended up in the playroom with 4-year-old Finn. His 1-year-old brother Patrick was sleeping upstairs and everyone was asked to play quietly so as not to wake him.

At one point Finn picked up one of his toy trucks, revved up the wheels, and let it roll across the playroom floor and smash into the wall.

Dad was not too pleased.

"Finn, I told you to be quiet," my son said to my grandson. "I don't want to hear that again."

Finn apologized and he went on showing me all his favorite trucks for about five minutes. At one point I rolled over on the floor and bumped the offending truck with my leg. Unfortunately, it still had some rev left in the wheels and it took off and smashed into the wall on the other side of the room.

Finn's dad was agitated and started walking toward the room. Four-year-old Finn looked me in the eye and knew I had committed the wrong. But he put his little hand on my shoulder and said, "Don't worry Grandpa, I've got this one."

Then he turned to his oncoming agitated father and said, "I'm sorry Dad. It was a mistake. I won't let it happen again."

My 4-year-old grandson was covering for me. He was willing to take the blame so his grandfather did not get barked at for making noise.

Finn didn't have to tell me that he loved me.

• During the same week there was yet another example of what pure love looks like.

My wife was at her parents' home at Inverness Golf and Country Club when our smallest dog took ill. The usually energetic pup wobbled and fell to the ground.

My wife's immediate fear was that one of the prescription pills that her parents are taking might have fallen to the ground and been eaten by the dog.

To put this in perspective, you need to know that my wife has a new car and it was just cleaned. She really, really likes a clean car.

And she really, really likes her dogs.

When the pup took ill, she immediately got both dogs in her clean car and started driving toward the vet's office. She called me on her telephone and was past hysterical.

Way past.

"He's dying, he's dying," she was yelling through her sobs. "What should I do?"

With all questions involving animals, my good friend Dr. K.C. Nayfield is the guy I call for advice.

So I called him on my desk phone while my wife continued talking on the cell phone.

K.C. answered and quickly spouted out some possibilities. But a telephone diagnosis was really impossible – he said – especially since we didn't even know if the pup had consumed a pill.

K.C. did say the dog's "blood sugar" could be out of whack and wanted to know how long it had been since he had eaten anything.

It had been a while.

I passed the information on to my wife who was still crying while driving to the vet's office. She had some dog food in the car and immediately retrieved it.

At this point things got a little more confusing.

"Is he eating the food?" I asked.

"Phaw. Phew. Phaw. Phew," my wife answered.

"I didn't understand that," I replied. "Calm down and tell me what's happening."

"Phaw. Phew. Phaw. Phew," is all I got in reply. This went on for about 5 minutes and I was pretty worried that the dog was dying and my wife was having some pretty serious issues herself.

I later learned that because the "lamb and soybean" special mix dog food was in large chunks, my wife made the executive decision that she had to put the food in her mouth, chew it up into smaller pieces, and then give it to the dog.

The dog ate the small chunks and began to feel better.

The "Phaw. Phew. Phaw. Phew," was not a new level of

communication; it turned out to the be the sound of my wife chewing the lamb and soybean special mix dog food into smaller chunks and then gagging and spitting it out onto the interior windshield of her newly cleaned car.

"That stuff really tastes awful," she later admitted.

My wife did not have to tell our dog that she loves him.

Chapter 21 - Sept. 9, 2012

WATCH OUT FOR
FAST-GROWING TREES

I WENT TO lunch the other day and ran into a tree.

My story is that the tree was not behind my car when I parked it at the Highlander Café on Citrus Avenue in Crystal River.

When I got back into the vehicle, the tree had miraculously grown 25 feet tall and positioned itself so my left rear bumper would take a direct hit. When the bumper hit the virgin tree, the contents of the cup of hot coffee in my right hand flew into the sky, bounced off the interior roof and landed in my lap.

There is never a good place for hot coffee to land once it exits its assigned container, but landing in the lap of a male driver who has just slammed his vehicle into a tree that did not exist a mere 60 minutes ago is a particularly bad conclusion.

I said many bad words that cannot be printed in the newspaper.

Did I mention this was all taking place during one of our Florida afternoon thunderstorms?

Well, it did.

To escape the scalding coffee that was pooling in my seat, I jumped from the vehicle into a blinding rain storm.

While the cool Florida rain was helping soothe the coffee-induced burning on important parts of my anatomy, a burst of lightning quickly convinced me that standing in 2 inches of water under a large tree that had just sprouted during the last 60 minutes was also not a good idea.

For safety's sake, I knew I needed to jump back into my now-dented vehicle with the coffee pooling in the driver's seat. My goal was to reach the passenger's seat.

Did I mention that I also purchased a sticky bun with my coffee from the nice folks at the Highlander Café? They make very nice desserts at the Highlander Café.

Now soaking wet, holding the scalded area of my anatomy, still saying very bad words that cannot be printed in a family newspaper, I dove over the driver's seat and landed directly on the sticky bun that was occupying the passenger seat.

When you drop 180-soaking-wet-pounds onto a sticky bun, it can do some really awful things. It did all of those awful things and then some.

As I drove home, I was wet, burned, had a dented car that I could only blame on a tree that miraculously grew during my lunch break, and had sticky bun on my glasses, in my hair and somehow down the front inside of my shirt.

To come totally clean with my personal hypocrisy, I went to a Chronicle editorial board meeting the next day where we discussed the important public issue of when to take the driver's license away from senior citizens who no longer have the ability to safely handle a vehicle.

I did not participate in that discussion and I did not write that editorial.

My car is in the repair shop as I write this, and the doctor said the burns did not cause any permanent damage, although he did say I have developed a new twitch in my right eye.

Chapter 22 - Feb. 4, 2012

CULTURAL INTRO JUST
A BIT TOO EARLY

IZZY MULLIGAN OF St. Augustine recently turned 6 years old.

She is beautiful, intelligent, articulate and mature. Did I mention she's my oldest granddaughter and I've already promised her a convertible on her 16th birthday?

I totally understand the problems of overindulging young people — but too bad — she's my granddaughter and she can do no wrong. It's her father's job to discipline her and send her to the "time out" corner. It's my job as grandfather to spoil her and watch her father (my son) attempt to cope.

Since her 16th birthday is 10 years off, we decided it was too early to purchase the convertible and we needed to come up with another idea for this year's birthday extravaganza.

It was my brilliant thought to introduce Izzy to a unique cultural experience. Since her father is a University of Miami graduate, we conspired to inject some Gator enthusiasm into Izzy and give her a cultural experience at the same time. The off-Broadway production of "My Fair

Lady" was playing at the Phillips Center on the University of Florida campus in Gainesville. I decided that having her grandparents take her and her 4-year-old brother, Finn, to the play was a great idea.

So I purchased the tickets.

Expensive tickets.

Along came the night, and Izzy got all fixed up in a nice dress and her new pair of boots. We had a relaxing dinner before the show and Izzy was delighted as we entered the Phillips Center. The fountains out front were all lit up and grownups were dressed in their finest.

It was an official formal event and Izzy's enthusiasm was obvious.

Did I mention the tickets were expensive?

We found our seats (the expensive ones) as the full orchestra warmed up and offered little snippets of the amazing music from "My Fair Lady."

We were all excited.

And then the play began.

I had conveniently forgotten that the characters in the first part of "My Fair Lady" spend all their time speaking in a very clipped English accent that even the English have trouble understanding.

But the music was grand, the set changes fast and the audience fully engaged.

Except, of course, for Izzy.

About 10 minutes into the play Izzy leaned over and said in a somewhat loud voice:

"This is boring."

"It gets better," I promised her. "Just hang in there and you'll love it."

Izzy, trusting her grandfather, and maybe remembering I was the guy who promised her the convertible on her 16th birthday, gave it another try.

For about two minutes.

That's when my beautiful, intelligent, articulate and mature grand-daughter took off her new pair of boots to see if the play would get any better if she listened to it barefoot.

It didn't.

She then decided to see if the entertainment value of the experience would improve if she pulled her new dress up over the top of her head.

That didn't help either.

But my barefoot, dress-on-top-of-the-head granddaughter was now starting to get as many laughs as the play.

For full impact, Izzy began to rock with discontent in her seat.

Did I mention these seats were expensive?

The intermission eventually came and we quickly headed off toward the exits. Neither Izzy nor Finn seemed to mind in the least that we left at half-time of our first official University of Florida event.

As we walked toward the car — perhaps searching for some positive feedback on the event — I asked Izzy what the favorite part of the show was.

She had no trouble coming up with a quick answer.

"The end," she said.

Our next cultural event is going to either involve mud and large trucks or include the word "Disney" in the title.

Chapter 23 - October 2012

AN UGLY TOE CAN MAKE
YOU IRRITATED

AS WE GET older, our bodies can let us down.

We can train them. Feed them. Starve them. Exercise them and even talk trash to them.

But they eventually let us down.

It's part of the cycle.

My eyes were the first to go. Things get a little blurry when I don't have my glasses on.

It can be very difficult to read tiny type.

Actually it was my toe that went first. Because of the bad eyes, I couldn't see the toe so I didn't realize anything was wrong.

I hurt my big toe on a sailing trip and eventually some sort of ugly fungus started growing on it.

Sure, that was ten years ago and now after a doctor told me to do something about it I have been using a very expensive medication that I am supposed to apply each day.

After reading the instructions on the label of the medication, the prescription scares me more than the ugly toe.

First they told me not to apply the medication in the bathroom.

Where the heck else am I supposed to put it on?

Does everyone else apply medications in the kitchen? The backyard?

Then the instructions told me to be careful because the medication is flammable. I should not apply the stuff near flames or cigarettes because I could explode.

I don't smoke, but the flame and explosion thing has me concerned.

Can my toe catch fire? You think the toe is ugly now, wait till we have a fire.

Right below the fire warning it tells me not to get the toe wet.

Now if the toe catches fire, can I get a special exemption and get the toe wet?

It doesn't tell me why I shouldn't get the toe wet, but the warning is pretty serious – DO NOT GET YOUR TOE WET.

The medication also does all the usual things that you expect from a modern day medication including making you dizzy, nauseous, unable to drive a car and in extreme cases – it can cause death.

For a toe.

I could die, but my toe would look better.

The medication can also make you irritated.

They will tell you around the office that I am already pretty irritated on a regular basis so maybe it would have the opposite effect on me and make me happy. Unless of course it caught fire or got wet. Then I would be irritated over the resulting explosion.

So back to the story of using the medication to fix the ugly appearance of my toe.

I applied the medication for about two months and absolutely nothing good happened. Each morning I went into the backyard and applied the stuff unless it was raining because - as you remember - I can't get the toe wet.

But the toe was still ugly.

In fact, I think it got uglier. But I have trouble seeing that far.

So I ask my darling wife for her opinion on the toe issue and this is where it goes back to the eyes.

She took one look at the toe medication and told me I was applying a nasal decongestant to my ugly toe. The real toe medication was in the other cabinet.

They make the print on the prescription bottle so small that I couldn't really read what the heck it said.

The written instructions said 'toe' but the bottle said 'nose'.

There is good news and bad news here.

The good news is that I never caught fire or got dizzy.

The other good news is that my toe never caught a cold or got congested.

The bad news is that I still have one ugly toe.

And bad eyes.

And now I am very irritated.

Chapter 24 - October 2012

THE WIND BLOWS IN
NEW EXPERIENCES

THE WIND WAS hollowing last Saturday morning in Crystal River. The rain was still falling and when I walked onto my back deck I could see that we had one of the highest tides in a very long time.

In fact, the river water was all the way up to the street and as high as it was with some of the hurricanes we had back in 2004. Small waves were breaking over the top of my dock.

Despite the weather and wind, it felt like a relaxing idea to enjoy a cup of coffee and experience Mother Nature in its rawest form.

What a wonderful way to start off a Saturday.

And then – "Holy Mackerel" - my boat was not sitting in the lift at the end of the dock.

Our brand new 20-ft. pontoon boat was gone.

It takes a few minutes for something like that to compute. When I went to bed my boat was there. Now it's gone.

I stood there in the wind and rain and just stared at the empty space hoping that it would appear.

It did not.

At first I thought the boat had been stolen. Based on the headlines in my own paper we've recently been experiencing a crime wave of sorts, so maybe some meth addict stole it and sold it for some quick drug money.

Hmm. That didn't feel right.

Then I thought that maybe county commission Chairman Scott Adams might have come and borrowed my boat to go do a tour of the proposed Port Citrus at the barge canal. Scott is always out doing some kind of fact finding work so I thought maybe he picked up Dixie Hollins and together they did a tour up the river.

Hmm. That didn't feel right either.

That's when a wave from the river broke over the top of dock and soaked my bedroom slippers. I looked at the wet slippers and then back at the boat lift.

Water, wind, waves? That's when it came to me – Mother Nature had stolen my boat.

For the record, I had yet to take that first relaxing drink of coffee.

The wind was coming at 25 knots from the west. I have never had a boat lift before and here's a little fact they didn't put in with the boat lift instruction manual.

If the tide comes in as high as your boat, and the wind is blowing at 25 knots, your boat is not hanging around for that first cup of coffee.

In a panic I ran inside and woke up my wife. "Our boat has gone out to sea without us," I boomed. "Let's get going."

We got in the car and began driving through Crystal River neighborhoods searching for the errant pontoon boat. I was dreading the telephone call to insurance agent Linda Van Allen to tell her that my boat was stolen by Mother Nature.

After searching for a while, I realized one nautical truism; our boat wouldn't be blown out to sea because the wind was blowing the wrong way. We went looking to the east toward Hunter Springs Park and areas beyond.

We bounced around the neighborhoods and I went climbing through the backyards of multiple condominiums and homes trying to get a glimpse of the missing boat. First, let me apologize for not stopping to explain to the woman in the bathrobe who I startled.

Yes, I may have looked like a mad man, but I was on a mission.

And to the snarling dog that tried to attach itself to my rear quarter – I may be old but I'm faster than I look when my life is on the line.

After another 30 minutes it was my wife who saw the escaped boat being carried into the backyard of a home at the east end of the Hunter Spring basin. I climbed through the backyards, pushed the boat back into the water and started the engine right up.

There were no scrapes or bruises on the boat and I can only hope it didn't crash into anyone else's boat along the river.

When you think you have a grip on what life is going to give you on any given day, real life gets in the way and disrupts the norm.

When I got back to my dock and tied up the boat (that is the key lesson here – you have to tie up the darn boat even if it is in lift) I sat down and finally took a sip of coffee.

It was cold.

I took that as a message and went back to bed.

Chapter 25 - March 2013

CELEBRATING BASEBALL HISTORY AND BIG ED

ED HEMSWORTH OF Inverness, who happens to be my father-in-law, turned 90 this week.

To celebrate his birthday, my wife decided to take him to a New York Yankees spring training game in Tampa.

In his time, Ed was a great baseball player. If not for World War II, he would have ended up playing at the major league level.

My darling wife thought it would be a great idea to ask the folks at Steinbrenner Field in Tampa to give a little recognition to Ed during one of those many breaks that take place during a baseball game.

One of the highlights of Ed's baseball career was he played for the Staten Island All Stars before WWII and one of his teammates was Bobby Thomson. Thomson later played for the New York Giants and was responsible for one of the most dramatic moments in baseball history.

It was 1951 when Thomson — known as the Staten Island Scot — hit the "Shot heard round the world" to win the National League pennant for the Giants. The Giants were playing the hated Brooklyn Dodgers and the 1951 season ended with the two New York teams tied. There was a three-game playoff between the teams. And after each side won once, the season went down to a winner-take-all game.

The final game was the first nationally televised sporting event. Think about that — this was the beginning of the nation coming together for a major sporting event on live TV.

In the bottom of the ninth inning, the Dodgers were ahead 4-2 when Thomson came to the plate. Two men were on base and Thomson hit a walk-off home run, winning the pennant for the Giants. Every baseball fan in America heard the Giants play-by-play announcer repeatedly yell "The Giants win the pennant. The Giants win the pennant" as Thomson ran around the bases. It was an immortal moment in sports.

This brings us back to 2013 when I am on the phone with the marketing department with the New York Yankees explaining the connection to Ed Hemsworth and his 90th birthday.

"He played on the All Star team with Bobby Thomson," I said.

"Who?" the young woman in the marketing department asked.

"Bobby Thomson, the Shot Heard Round the World," I said.

"Could you spell that," she asked.

Hmmm. This wasn't working. She did not know who Bobby Thomson was, so there wasn't much chance we were going to get a shout out at the stadium. The young lady was really nice, but she told me there lots of important things to announce during a game and the spots had already been filled.

So here's my own "shout-out" for Ed Hemsworth of Inverness, Fla. He was a really good baseball player who attended St. Michael's College in Vermont where he also played basketball. At the end of his sophomore year in 1943, he joined the Navy and like most other young men of his generation joined the war effort.

At least one major league team expressed an interest in calling Ed to play baseball in the Big Time, but the priority of war and family got in the way.

Bobby Thomson, who died a few years ago, will always be remembered as a hero for the "Shot heard round the world." But guys like Ed Hemsworth — who let a war get in the way of his personal opportunities — will always be a hero to me.

The folks at Steinbrenner Field might not remember what Bobby Thomson and Ed Hemsworth did for this country, but we do.

And here's the final chapter. My darling wife was not about to let baseball ignore her father. When she went to the Yankee-Red Sox game Wednesday she brought along a poster that congratulated her Dad for his 90th birthday. She went down and waved the poster in front of her section and the crowd sang "Happy Birthday" to Ed Hemsworth.

Chapter 26 - July 7, 2013

~~~

THE RAIN KEEPS COMING
AND SO DO THE SNAKES

IF YOU WANT to know why it seems to be raining every day for the last three weeks, I've been sitting on the answer.

I purchased a rain barrel.

That's right, a rain barrel.

My wife volunteers on the city water board in Crystal River, and we've become very aware of how valuable water is for the future of our area. So we don't waste water.

I routinely get pleasant reminders that I should not leave the water on when I'm brushing my teeth and I should take shorter showers.

We have lived in our house for eight years and I have never watered the front lawn. I'd like to say this is because I am very dedicated to protecting our water supply, but it's really because I'm lazy.

But the grass is green and it looks fine. So why bother?

Anyway, back to the rain barrel. I went out three weeks ago and purchased the rain barrel for the flowers we have around the house. I actually had some good folks come by and install a short gutter on the garage roof so I could capture the rain directly into my new rain barrel.

After having everything installed, I was happy to see that it immediately rained and filled up my rain barrel.

The next day it rained again and my rain barrel overflowed.

The next day it rained again and my rain barrel overflowed again.

And every day since that day, it has rained in Citrus County.

My rain barrel flows over each day and the rain just keeps coming.

Some of my flowers are now dying from water rot.

I am going home tonight and kicking over the rain barrel to see if I can make the rain stop. I'll let you know how it goes.

One effect of too much rain is that the snakes of Citrus County are become displaced.

Snakes like to snuggle up in dry, enclosed places after they've eaten a meal. Because of the above-mentioned rain, the regular dry places are now a foot underwater.

So all over Citrus County, snakes are looking for new homes.

Which brings me to my garage.

We had an electrician in a week ago on a project (not the rain barrel) and he told me he saw a very large snake in our garage. He stretched his arms and said it was at least six feet long.

Then he made a circle with his two hands and said it was fat as my leg.

That sounded like a big snake.

So I went into the garage looking for the snake.

I wasn't sure why I was actually looking for the snake because if I found it, it would only create the new dilemma of what the heck to do with it.

A six-foot snake as fat as my leg doesn't sound like something I really wanted to fool with. If I was actually successful in finding the snake, the most aggressive thing I could do was to politely ask it to leave.

"Please, Mr. Snake. Go visit my neighbor Jim's house because he enjoys the company," I would say. (Jim is a lawyer; he's used to hanging around snakes. He also has several large guns.) But after knocking around in the garage for 10 minutes I couldn't find the fat, six-foot long snake.

In a moment of relief, I put my right hand down on the top of my golf bag and thought about putting them in the back of my car. At that exact moment Mr. Fat Snake introduced himself.

He had wrapped himself inside my golf bag and around my five-iron. His entire body was in the golf bag and only his Fat Snake head stuck out.

I thought it was the six-iron.

In my best imitation of a school girl, I screamed and whooped and hollered and danced.

I have not danced in a long time, and my performance obviously traumatized the snake.

He quickly exited the golf bag and went back under the house.

I am going to treat the snake just like county government treats its budget deficit. I'm going to make believe it's not there and hope it goes away.

Chapter 27 - Feb. 1, 2014

———— ∞ ————

MR. LARSON WAS NOT
COMING HOME

WHEN I STARTED in the newspaper business, no one was really interested in my opinion on too much.

They just wanted to be sure that I delivered the newspaper to my 44 customers before <u>4:30 p.m.</u> and that I placed each copy of Newsday as close to the front door as possible.

I was not a great delivery boy, but the job experience was my first in this business, and I consider myself fortunate to still have incredible passion for it today.

My experience as a newspaper boy came roaring back to me last week when I read the Chronicle story of 79-year-old Cecylia Ziobro Thibault.

Cecylia survived a Nazi forced labor camp and recently contributed to a book, written by her son Robert, about her experiences as a slave laborer. She was compelled to tell her story at this late date because the president of Iran has repeatedly proclaimed that the Holocaust is a hoax. Mrs. Thibault knew it was not a hoax; she lived through the horrors.

When I delivered Newsday to those 44 customers on Cedar Road in East Northport, N.Y., I learned that the world was made up of very different people. Some people were nice; others weren't.

Some were grateful for your hard work; others were always quick to point out that your efforts needed improvement.

"Why don't you put the paper inside the screen door?" one would say.

"Why don't you get here earlier?" another would ask. To an 11-year-old kid, the complaints turned to cynicism when you discovered the only time the complaining customers were not around was when you needed to do your weekly collection.

We had to go door to door on Friday and get 25 cents from each customer.

It was brutal. I could often hear the television inside the house, but the people wouldn't answer the door.

They didn't want to turn 25 cents over to the 11-year-old kid who had very little experience as a bill collector and some weeks seemed to be working hard just to break even.

But when you're 11 years old, you remember the good people. The ones who treated you with respect.

And that brings me to Mrs. Larson, the second to last house on my route.

Mrs. Larson was my best tipper. She gave me 50 cents a week and was always so grateful to see me.

Each Friday I would stop at her house and she would invite me inside for some home-made cookies. She was an elderly woman and she spoke with a thick accent I was not familiar with.

She lived alone and never had company.

There was a photo of a young Mrs. Larson with her husband that sat on the fireplace. He was dressed in a funny-looking suit and had a big mustache.

I would always ask Mrs. Larson when her husband was coming home. She would just tell me "Soon. He's coming home soon."

I never met Mrs. Larson's husband, and as an 11-year-old, I thought he must have had an awful job, because he was never around.

"He's coming home soon," Mrs. Larson would tell me.

One summer day I came to the house and she invited me inside for my regular cookies and 50 cents. It was hot and she was wearing a short-sleeved blouse.

That's when I noticed the funny numbers on the inside of her wrist.

I was a dopey 11-year-old kid and did not understand. I asked her why she had the numbers on her wrist, and she got embarrassed and tried to hide them.

I didn't understand.

That's when she told me that she once lived in a very bad place where they did not like people like her. She was Jewish.

I didn't know what that meant. I thought everyone was a Catholic.

She told me she lived in a camp with thousands of other people just like her. In the camp, she said, everyone had their own number put on their wrists.

At the camp, she got separated from her husband.

She loved Americans, Mrs. Larson told me, because they freed her from the camp and let her come to this country. She had searched and searched for her husband, but never found him.

But she was sure he was still looking for her. As she said it, she looked out the curtains of her living room to see if anyone was coming. To see if her husband had come home.

This was in 1964. The war had ended in 1945.

Mr. Larson was not coming home.

I was a stupid 11-year-old kid and did not understand.

But today I do understand. And when I hear the president of Iran mouth off that the Holocaust was a myth, I want him to have to sit in

Mrs. Larson's living room, eat her cookies and explain why Mr. Larson never came home.

Cecylia Ziobro Thiabault and her son have written a book that I will read.

And none of us should ever forget how evil people can become.

Chapter 28 - Oct. 4, 2014

GET THE SCIENTISTS TO WHIP ME UP AN OREO TREE

I WAS DISCOURAGED to find out recently that Oreo cookies are not part of a healthy diet. After 50 years of eating an Oreo every day, I was advised by a doctor friend that the old saying was "An apple a day keeps the doctor away," and that Oreo can not be interchanged at will.

I must have missed that story, because I swear it was Oreos.

Anyway, the advice got me thinking that just maybe I should work more fruit into my diet.

So a few weeks back I went on a diet that included a daily intake of oranges, apples, grapes, raisins. Better late than never, I concluded.

Fruit would be good for me. I would have more energy. Play better tennis and probably be a nicer person, to boot.

Tennis is one of my main ways of staying active. Several times a week after work I will meet with some friends at the local tennis courts to play.

My problem has been that after working for nine or 10 hours and then going off to the tennis courts, I would often lose energy in the middle of the match.

For many years I had been bringing along a few Oreo cookies, but they no longer seemed to be working.

Fruit was the obvious answer. I had to slip some fruit into my tennis bag each morning to give me some extra energy halfway through my two-and-half-hour tennis match.

I first tried to bring a banana, but I soon discovered that if you let a banana sit in the trunk of a car in the hot Florida sun for nine hours most of its nutritional value turns to mush.

Raisins seemed like the obvious answer. They come in a nice package and are already dried up and wrinkled.

So earlier this week I went off to the tennis courts with a package of raisins in the bag.

Now, mind you, I don't play tennis with a bunch of wimpy guys; we're pretty serious about our sport. One of my opponents, Jerry Boley of Inverness, is an official over at the federal prison in Sumter County. He hangs out all day with murderers, kidnappers and the occasional terrorist, so he has been known to occasionally have a bad attitude about losing.

"I had to quell a riot in A Block today and then tell a murderer that his 14th request for early release had been denied," Boley would say. "What did you do at work?"

"Hmmm. I went to a meeting and got barked at by Scott Adams," I replied.

My day didn't seem to match up in the tough-guy category, but what the heck.

So that brings me to the raisins at my Tuesday night tennis match.

About half way through the match, I was running out of steam and went to my bag for my secret weapon.

I popped out the raisins, took a handful and tossed them in my mouth.

I tried to look tough, but that's difficult with raisins.

After walking back onto the court and munching my raisins, I got a strange feeling on my hands and arms.

I looked down and there were hundreds of raisins running up and down my arms.

After a closer look, and a few bites, it became obvious that the raisins had somehow become ants.

I've never had this problem with Oreos.

While I continued to munch the raisins in my mouth, I threw my tennis racket to the ground and begin to wildly wipe the ants off my hands and arms. I may or may not have squealed like a 9-year-old.

Did I mention that I was still chewing?

About that time my tongue began to send signals to the brain which said "WARNING! WARNING!"

My tongue was on fire and a thousand ants — impersonating raisins — were feasting on the inside of my mouth.

For the uninitiated, tennis has a lot of rules. If you violate the rules, you lose a point. If you violate more rules, you lose the game.

I began spitting and barfing up the mouth invaders while I rolled around on the court and occasionally said bad words.

All of these actions are against the rules, but my life was in the balance and I didn't care.

It took 10 minutes of rinsing my mouth with water and spitting to be rid of the intruders. My hands and arms were covered with bites. My mouth was still on fire as I sat on the bench trying to regain enough composure to continue to play.

Prison guy Boley walked over and very empathetically said: "I stopped a riot in A Block today. Get out here and play more tennis."

My fruit campaign has ended. My tennis bag will only carry Oreos going forward.

Chapter 29 - Dec. 6, 2014

A PEACEFUL MESSAGE FROM
A FEATHERED 'FRIEND'

SOMETIMES OMENS JUST fall from the sky. The most peaceful moment of my day usually happens first thing in the morning when I get a hot cup of coffee and go outside and sit on the dock.

I usually bring the newspaper, but first I just sit and admire what Mother Nature has in store for Citrus County. Birds, manatees, the occasional dolphin all greet me as the sun begins to make its daily climb into the sky.

Sounds peaceful, huh? Well, not always.

I was sitting on said dock last week admiring the first whisper of dawn. The air was cold and the coffee was hot.

I felt an inner peace.

A flock of gulls flew over me and I listened for the rhythmic flapping of their wings.

That's when I heard a loud "plunk" and got splashed by my coffee. You know what else birds can do while they fly? They poop.

And that's exactly what this selfish gull dropped right into my coffee cup.

She then (of course it had to be a female gull) landed in my backyard to triumphantly squawk at me and my now-polluted coffee.

Being a true red-blooded American, I decided the gull needed her neck strangled for this broadside attack on my peaceful morning.

Just like that, I went from being "one with nature" to wanting to wring the neck of the offending bird. Classic passive-aggressive behavior runs deep in my family.

I moved swiftly down the dock in my Jim Bowie slippers, snuck down the steps and anticipated the taste of sea gull soup.

That's about the time the Jim Bowie slippers failed me and my legs went flying toward the heavens. As Rotarian Doug Lobel knows from his rib-cracking kayak experience of two years ago, the mud along the tidal river in my backyard gets pretty darn slippery.

The poop-contaminated coffee cup was still in my hand and the previously described polluted contents made their way toward the heavens.

Since the Earth's gravitational pull is still very strong in the morning, my flying through the air had a predictable conclusion. Led by my rear quarters, I splashed into the river mud.

That graceless thump was followed very quickly by the Earthbound return of the hot coffee containing the bird poop. As I lay on my back, the contaminated concoction of course could only land in one place, and that was all over the front of my shirt.

The offending gull didn't move a feather while I checked to make sure that none of my extremities were broken or bent the wrong way.

The gull looked at me and said, "Squawk."

In bird language, that means, "No soup for you."

Chapter 30 - May 2, 2015

Chapter 30 - May 2, 2015

~∞~

BEING NICE MEANS PUTTING YOUR BEST FOOT FORWARD

I HAVE BAD feet.

When my feet hurt, I am not a nice person.

When I am not a nice person and a county commissioner calls up to complain, I tell him to "grow up and stop complaining."

When I tell a county commissioner to "grow up and stop complaining," my newspaper usually gets blistered at the next county commission meeting and everyone wonders what the heck happened.

It's because I have bad feet.

A while back I found a pair of shoes that gave me great relief. They are size-10 black Crocs that are made to look like dress shoes. I can wear them to work and they look like regular shoes. The secret is that they feel like bedroom slippers.

For many months I was a very nice person and didn't bark at any politicians. Even Scott Adams began to believe I was a nice guy.

Then last summer I went to my niece's wedding in New York and brought my favorite shoes with me. We stayed all night at the wedding, danced to the music and had great fun.

We flew home the next day and when I unpacked I only had one shoe.

My feet immediately began to hurt.

I called the New York hotel and asked them to search for my one shoe — size 10, black Croc.

They hesitantly complied, but found no shoe.

My next step was to visit the Croc store to buy another pair. The clerk told me "No one buys them anymore, we sold out."

I wanted to hit him with Yogi's catcher's mitt.

Back home I checked the Croc website for my super-comfortable, pain-reducing size-10 black Croc. Sure enough, Croc stopped making the bedroom slipper that looks like a work shoe.

Within a week I had complaints from two county commissioners, one city councilmen and a sheriff each wondering why I was no longer a nice person.

I seriously thought about wearing just the one remaining shoe to work and using a real bedroom slipper on the other foot. I figured that half a bad person was better than a totally bad person.

My wife wouldn't let me out of the house.

So if you ran into me around the holidays and wondered why I didn't appear to be a nice person any longer, it was because my feet hurt and my shoes were just not getting the job done.

Last month I had to fly back to New York and I found myself driving past the very hotel where we stayed for the wedding. I flipped the car around and headed back for a rescue mission of one size-10 black Croc.

I went right to the front desk and said "I'm here for my shoe. Size 10, black Croc."

"And when did you lose the shoe?" the hotel clerk asked in a clipped

British accent. (I am not sure why a clerk with a British accent was working behind the counter at a Long Island hotel, but he may have been sent by central casting just to annoy me).

"It was about nine months ago," I said.

A thin smile eased across his lips. "We discard lost items after 60 days," he said with great pleasure. "We give everything to Goodwill."

I wasn't buying it.

"Show me the lost-and-found items," I demanded. "Or I'm not leaving."

"Help yourself," he said and directed me to a room down the hall.

It was not a lost-and-found box; it was a lost-and-found room. And it was filled with everything you could imagine: Musical instruments, cosmetics, an electric toothbrush, a broom and 42 different telephone chargers. There were books, crayons, a painting of a seascape and all sorts of clothes. And shoes. Many, many shoes.

But after an hour of searching, no size-10 black Croc.

I had traveled more than 1,000 miles for the rescue, but I went home feeling like President Jimmy Carter after the helicopters went down in that blasted sandstorm.

I returned to Florida with aching feet and no hope in sight.

Fast forward to last Monday, when my wife called the office to tell me what she had found in a suitcase stuffed in the attic.

"It's a size-10 black Croc, and there is only one of them," she said.

I once was lost, but now I'm found. Blind but now I see.

I endured nine months of pain and my size-10 black Croc suddenly appears.

My theory is that Commissioner Scott Adams figured out why I was being so mean and searched through his landfill in Sumter County until he found a discarded size-10 black Croc. He then snuck it into that suitcase in my attic so I would find it, reduce my foot pain and once again become a nice person.

My wife suggested I might have unpacked too quickly after the wedding and further proposed that I stop reading so many detective novels.

All I know is that life is good again.

Chapter 31 - October 2015

"It doesn't get any better than this"

In August we gathered a bunch of friends and family to go watch a Tampa Bay Rays' game down in St. Petersburg. The New York Mets were in town and I have been a fan of the Mets since 1962 when the hapless team got its start at the Polo Grounds, the old Giant's stadium in New York.

There was not a legacy of baseball in my family, but I got hooked on the game early because my little league coach used to take us stragglers along to see the Mets play.

With seven kids in our family, there wasn't much time for pushing kids into sports or going to a professional baseball game.

My older brother and I both joined little league, but we were on our own – as were most kids at the time. Parents never attended a single game and even in the second grade we rode our bikes to the ball field.

We wanted to play baseball and we figured out how to make it happen.

I was never the best baseball player on our team – but I was always the dirtiest.

In the beginning I played second base and was always diving for groundballs. Even if they were hit on the other side of the infield.

I just liked diving into the dirt. (This could explain my later decision to go into newspapering.)

The coach eventually decided to make me a catcher because the catcher plays close to the ground and was expected to get dirty.

I have tried hard to help my own family enjoy playing and watching baseball. My wife and I managed a little league team in Inverness in the 1980s and all the kids played.

One of the first professional games we took our four kids to was a Mets game at Shea Stadium in New York. We traveled all the way to Shea and when we parked the car I said: "Don't forget the tickets."

My wife said: "I thought you brought the tickets."

The Mets' tickets were still sitting on our kitchen table back in Florida.

Fortunately, the marketing team at Shea Stadium loved our sob story and gave us seats to watch the game.

All of my extended family of brothers, sisters, cousins, nephews, nieces and in-laws are Yankee fans. Everyone loves the Yankees because they are winners. I loved the Mets because they were losers and they needed someone to care.

That's also why over the years I have used birthdays and Christmas as a time to send Mets' hats or shirts to nieces and nephews around the country. I have tried to nurture defection from all those Yankee loving families.

In their very first season, the Mets lost 120 games, the worst performance since the Boston Braves in 1935. They were 60.5 games out of first place.

The Mets needed love. And better players.

When we visited Tropicana Field for the Rays/Mets game in August, it was the first visit to a professional ballgame for some of the grandchildren. They have visited many professional soccer games, because that is becoming the sport of this next generation.

I keep working on sparking a love of baseball and the Mets.

Patrick Mulligan, 5, of St. Augustine was sitting in a good seat with his Mets shirt on, a hotdog in one hand and a drink in the other. "Grandpa, it doesn't get better than this," he told me.

He's a smart kid.

The Mets lost to the Rays that day, but they went on to win their division and a place in the playoffs. As all baseball fans know, the Mets defeated the Dodgers in the first round and then swept the Cubs on Wednesday to win the National League pennant.

It's on to the World Series and the grandkids are staying up to watch the early innings of the game. Loyal Mets' fans hope that it's the beginning of a dynasty.

And grandfathers hope it's the germination of the next crop of baseball fans. Because as Patrick said, "It doesn't get any better than this."

Chapter 32- May 2016

WE PASS DOWN THE SKILLS
AND WEAKNESSES

I AM NOT a great cook, but I am good eater.

One of the most disappointing moments of being a father came on August 7, 1988 when my oldest son suggested that my hamburgers cooked on the grill tasted like hockey pucks.

"How do you know what a hockey puck tastes like," I would ask. "You live in the south."

"They taste bad," my son replied. "That's all I know."

Children don't lie about food. If they don't like what you put in front of them, they're going to let you know.

One of the reasons I always liked President George W. Bush is that we shared a hatred of broccoli. His mother forced him to eat broccoli and so did mine.

I can not lie about broccoli – it's awful. Sorry broccoli farmers, I can't fake it. Why don't you try growing corn or baked beans?

My kids couldn't lie about my hamburgers – they were bad. And this was coming from kids who loved hamburgers.

I did have a tendency to overcook the patties because I feared an undercooked burger would get one of the kids sick.

"Don't worry about that," the oldest boy would always say. "We don't eat your burgers so we won't get sick."

I should have fed them broccoli instead.

Anyway, it was with great joy that I was visiting this same oldest son recently at his home in St. Augustine Beach. He is now an attorney practicing law with some big firm and he is used to people listening to his advice.

We were having a barbecue to celebrate the birthday of his oldest child, 9-year-old Izzy Mulligan.

While we sat around eating the burgers and hotdogs, HIS oldest son – Finn - walked through the room and said: "I think I'll have a hot dog, I hate your hamburgers, Dad."

There it was – the circle of life right in front of me.

I tried not to say anything, but my grandson's burger hating comments set off the bells of Notre Dame in my ears. A smile crossed my face and my son immediately gave me the evil eye.

My failures as a cooking father weren't just my failures – they were the failure of my gene pool.

Not only had I taught my son how to throw a baseball and argue a political point of view – I had also taught him how to grill a bad burger.

History became clear to me. My father grilled a bad burger. There were seven brothers and sisters in my family so it took a long time to get things off the grill. Most of them were burnt.

I spent my childhood eating bad burgers.

And then I did the same thing to my children.

And now my children are doing it to their children.

Life suddenly has a deeper meaning.

We pass many things along to our children, and not all of them are good.

Finn came back inside and sat with me while he ate his hot dog. Finn is a sweet boy who would never do anything to hurt the feelings of his own father.

He just spoke the truth as he saw it.

I could see Finn in 30 years having his own backyard barbecue and feeding his own children 'hockey puck' hamburgers.

It was at that moment of clarity that it felt right to offer some grandfatherly advice to Finn.

"Son," I said, "stick with the hot dogs. It's tougher to mess them up."

Chapter 33 - May 2016

LOOKING FOR FREEDOM
IN THE MIRROR

As FATHER'S DAY is right around the corner, I have special dispensation to tell you about one of my wife's really strange habits.

She loves the great outdoors. She loves the great outdoors so much that while she is in the house she likes to leave the doors open.

Wide open.

Never mind that we have big windows and screened porches that make it feel like you're outdoors. She prefers to be really outdoors.

We live in a neighborhood where it is not unusual to see osprey, alligators, raccoons, squirrels, lizards, owls, snakes, two dozen species of birds and other assorted wildlife prowling around.

I constantly advise her that if she keeps leaving the doors open, she will one day find some wild animal sitting in the living room watching HDTV. She responds that she wouldn't mind the company as I refuse to sit and watch HDTV with her.

You get the picture - we are happily married.

Usually, when she sees me pull my car into the driveway, she will close the doors in an effort to avoid the inevitable confrontation that her strange behavior and my know-it-all personality will produce.

So last Monday when I stopped by the house after lunch I was not surprised that all the doors were closed - even though the house had that "outside" smell to it.

When I went into the bathroom in the master bedroom I was chagrined to find the place a mess. Towels and toiletries were thrown all over the place and there was goopy stuff all of my counter-top.

Her counter-top was clean.

My counter-top had piles of this unidentified goop all over it.

I did what any other guy would do – I stuck my hand in the goop and smelled it.

It didn't smell like anything I had smelled before – and it was not pleasant.

My first paranoid thought was that Sen. Charlie Dean had somehow gotten into my house and trashed my bathroom in retaliation for our last "barn" editorial. The goop smelled like it came from a barn – even a barn with three bedrooms and a kitchen.

With goop dripping from my finger, I went looking for my wife.

"What happened to the bathroom and what is this stuff," I asked.

She took a deep breath and used a classic diversionary tactic. "Have you seen my latest art work."

"The goop," I said with finger outstretched. "What is it?"

"Well, I guess I didn't tell you about the birds," she replied.

"The birds," I asked.

It seems that the porch doors were left in their customary wide-open position when some birds flew in the house. My wife went looking for them, but they were tricky birds and went into hiding.

It was sometime later that she heard the thumping coming from our bathroom and she went to investigate.

One of the birds had managed to find the mirror above my

counter-top and he was sure the reflection of sunshine represented freedom. So he proceeded to fly with all his might into the mirror.

Each time he did so, he apparently had a "pooping" experience.

Hence, the large piles of bird poop on my counter.

I was at least relieved that Sen. Dean had not breached our security.

Less you think that any lessons were learned through the ordeal, my wife explained that it took her 45 minutes to capture the flying winged, bipedal, endothermic (warm-blooded), vertebrate 'poop' machine that was fouling up my bathroom counter.

She finally got a clothes' basket and trapped the creature against the mirror. She held the basket closed and carried the frightened animal back out on the porch to set it free.

This did not turn out to be one of those "Free Willy" moments where the bird flies off to freedom.

"Why" you may ask? Well, because my wife still had the house doors propped open.

As soon as she let the bird out of the basket the dumb thing flew back in the house and raced to my bathroom mirror where he proceeded to bang his head and drop additional poop on my counter.

I guess I can at least be happy that it wasn't an alligator.

Chapter 34 - June 4, 2016

-------◆◆◆-------

SOME UPDATED MEDICAL TRAINING IS ON THE PRIORITY LIST

LIFE CHANGES IN the blink of an eye.

I was unloading surfboards and luggage from my car for a Memorial Day visit to my son's home in St. Augustine Beach. The weather was perfect, the waves were nice, the wind was from the west and the grandkids were delighted to see us.

We were ready for a break.

As I reached up to the roof to pull a strap from the car, a water moccasin darted from under a bush near the driveway and latched on to the instep of my right foot. The poisonous snake – sometimes called a Cottonmouth – jabbed its fangs deep into my flesh.

I didn't see the snake until I was shaking my foot trying to dislodge it. Izzy, my 10-year-old granddaughter, was standing right next to me and she let out a yelp.

She had never heard her grandfather use such language.

Instantly I knew the snake was poisonous, even though it slithered back into the bush before I had a clear view.

My first thought was that Izzy was safe. The second thought was that I had never felt pain like this before.

As I fell to the ground in agony, my extensive medical training kicked in.

I was a Boy Scout back in the 1960s and they taught us how to deal with snake bites. Earning the First Aid merit badge was about to pay off.

Did I mention the training was from the 1960s?

First, I demanded that my wife not lose eye contact with the snake. "It's in the bush," I yelled in between unprintable expletives. "Don't lose it."

Then I ordered my son to get a razor blade. "Quick, get a straight razor if you have it," I insisted.

I am good at giving orders.

As my son dialed 911, he looked on in that disbelieving way that only a son can have for a father. "Why does he want to shave now?" was obviously the thought running through his head.

Through my yelps of pain I explained that in the Scouts they taught us to use the razor blade to cut into the skin between the two fang marks and open up a wound.

Once bleeding, the process called for me to use my mouth to suck the venom out of injured instep and spit it onto the ground.

That would explain why I was lying on the front lawn in this nice residential neighborhood trying to bend my leg around the back of my neck so I could get the instep into my mouth.

I was stuck in a contorted yoga position while still creating new versions of old bad words.

"That sounds like a really bad idea," my son told me while he simultaneously gave directions to the 911 dispatcher.

"Get me a razor," I demanded.

He ran back into the house looking for a razor, or at least humoring me.

"Can't find anything," he yelled from the inside the house.

Miraculously, the city police department was on the scene in four minutes and the EMS wagon was just 60 seconds behind them.

The place was crawling with rescue folks and thanks to the diligent effort of my wife, they found the snake and determined the species.

That's when my son asked the trained EMS folks about my demands for the razor.

It's not helpful for rescue personal to laugh when they are saving a life, but some of the guys couldn't help themselves.

"Let me guess," one of them asked. "You were a Boy Scout."

"Be prepared," I told them.

"Debunked 30 years ago," the EMS guy replied.

Hmmm. Some updating of my limited medical training is probably in order.

The very competent rescue personnel got me to Flagler Hospital in less than 20 minutes from our 911 call and that was critical. The hospital happened to have the anti-venom in stock and it took 16 vials of it pumped into my arm before I was stabilized.

(Just a few months before a snake bite victim was taken to the same hospital and there was no anti-venom in stock. The victim was flown out by helicopter to Jacksonville but he later lost his leg from the poison.)

While it was a miserable Memorial Day weekend, luck really was on my side. My granddaughter was not bitten; I could not get my foot in my mouth; my son could not find a razor blade; my wife kept the snake in view; the emergency response folks were fast and good; the anti-venom was in stock; and the hospital staff was excellent.

I am thankful.

* In this very complicated world there are sometimes acts of human kindness that just take your breath away. In the pre-dawn hours of a day that I lost track of, I was in my hospital bed in the darkened room.

While I was heavily sedated, the pain was still throbbing.

As I began to wake, I felt a soothing motion against my swollen foot.

When I looked to the end of the bed, a veteran nurse was sitting in the darkness gently rubbing the puncture wound where the water moccasin had emptied its venom into my body.

"I thought this would make you feel better," she told me.

I told her it did.

Boy Scouts are not supposed to cry, so I hid the tears.

Chapter 35 - June 25, 2016

THE AFTERMATH OF THE

SNAKE ENCOUNTER

IT IS VERY appropriate that I got bit by a snake during election season.

Snakes always come out of the grass for elections.

The water moccasin that secured its fangs into the underside of my foot was deceitful and hiding in the dark. He just wanted to inflict pain and slither away into the grass.

My previous experience with snakes has been the political kind. In Florida we usually find the biggest snake and then elect them to public office.

I was humbled by the outpouring of concern from readers and friends after my encounter with the poisonous water moccasin. I have full use of my leg back and have heard first hand testimony of many people who suffered far more than I did when bitten.

True, not everyone was concerned about my recovery. Former county commissioner Jim Fowler left a message that he was very concerned about the snake.

Three or four readers joined in and suggested they were concerned the snake might have gotten food poisoning by coming in contact with my blood.

I have also heard from Boy Scouts around the country that never got the memo or email that using a razor blade on a snake bite was no longer the proper protocol for removing the venom of a poisonous snake.

One friendly reader did send a razor blade with a nice note scratched out in black crayon. There were lots of misspellings.

I think it came from the courthouse in Inverness.

Katie Myers, the head of marketing at Citrus Memorial Hospital, sent some very useful snake bite information along with this plea.

"The only important thing … is that nobody in the ER wants you to bring a dead snake/bobcat/whatever bit you into the hospital," suggested Ms. Myers.

For the record, I did not bring the live snake into Flagler Hospital. It was the police officer who caught the snake who brought it in.

The advice on snake bites from Ms. Myers was very helpful. It warns that if you get bit by a snake:

- Don't use a tourniquet.
- Don't drink or apply alcohol.
- Don't cut or suck the wound (the Boy Scout method from the 1960s).
- Don't apply ice.
- Don't try to catch the snake, kill the snake or touch the snake after you kill it. (This assumes you are not paying attention to these rules. You have to catch the snake to touch the snake).
- And most importantly, don't elect the snake to the Legislature. (I made that up, but it is very appropriate).
- If you are bitten by a snake, the 2016 rules are:
- Remain calm. (Easier said than done.)
- Immediately call 911.

- Limit movement and immobilize the bite area.
- Keep affected area at or below the heart. (That is if you have a heart. In Jim Fowler's case it might be difficult to find it).
- Remove jewelry and rings because you are about to swell up like a hippo.
- Try to safely observe the snake from a distance. (Tell the snake you will vote for it in the next election if it stays put until the 911 guys arrive. It is okay to lie to a snake. Remember, they were in the Garden of Eden and they were playing for the other team.)

Florida is filled with animals that would love to inflict a little pain. It is critical to understand the guidelines offered by Ms. Myers so you don't have to suffer any more than necessary.

My own family used the snake biting incident to supply me with the perfect Father's Day gift. I got my own pair of white Homosassa fishing boots to wear any time I leave the house and go into snake territory.

While wearing the boots I am safe and making a very impressive fashion statement at the same time.

Chapter 36 - Nov. 2016

DOG GETS HIS TREAT
AND THE LAST LAUGH

WE ALL KNOW that in general, a man is smarter than a dog.

No one told my dog.

For 12 years I have shared our household with Wilson — a somewhat neurotic Yorkie.

We have developed a ritual. He goes to the front door of our house and issues one short bark.

I get out of my seat, pick him up and carry him down the 13 steps to the front yard so he can do his duty.

Our house is in a flood zone, so we are 11 feet off the ground. For many years, Wilson would run down the steep 13 steps, do his business, and then run right back up.

Those were the Clinton years.

Now that we are nearing the end of the Obama years, Wilson requires his own form of Obamacare in that I must carry him down the 13 steps. His legs just don't have the bounce anymore.

Once he performs his digestive duty, he walks over to the stairs and gives me a sad look until I pick him up for the ride up the 13 steps.

If I am slow to retrieve him, he gives a short bark.

When we get back into the house, we together walk to the kitchen and he gets a treat. His 11-year-old brother, a 2-pound Yorkie, sits waiting at the top of the 13 steps because he is more interested in the treat than he is relieving himself.

He's no fool.

For my part in this exercise, I get nothing, except the actual exercise of walking up and down the 13 steps.

I do get the satisfaction in knowing that Wilson did not conduct his digestive duty in some hidden corner of the house.

We are very traditional in this ritual. Wilson will not go out the back door or the garage door; it must be the front door and the 13 steps.

In recent months, I have noticed that our trips up and down those 13 steps have become more regular. I figured his kidneys were beginning to fail and he simply had to go more frequently.

I had been going up and down the 13 steps with such frequency that my thighs were bulking up from the exertion. Five times a night, 13 steps coming and 13 steps going and then the treat.

Wilson recently made a trip to the veterinarian ,who said his health looked fine, including his kidneys — except for one factor.

He was gaining weight.

A lot of weight.

His meal routine hadn't changed, so it was hard to figure out.

The very next evening, I decided it was time to check a hunch.

After my third trip down the 13 steps, I decided a closer inspection was needed. When we got to the bottom of the stairs and Wilson raised his leg, I threw myself to the ground to get a better view of what was happening — or, as it would be, not happening.

Sure, the neighbors happened to be walking by while I had my stomach flat to the ground trying to sneak a peek under the 8-pound Yorkie, but I lost my pride a long time ago.

I was not going to be deterred.

Sure enough, my hunch was right. There was no fluid leaving the station. Instead, what I was participating in was a treat charade.

While I thought I had trained Wilson, it was the pudgy Yorkie who had trained me.

He had figured out that if he walked to the front door and barked, I would come over, pick him up and carry him down the 13 steps. Once I walked back up the 13 steps, he would get a treat.

What a great world — the human guy does all the work and the dog gets the treat.

We now have a truce in place.

Wilson walks to the front door and barks.

I throw him a treat.

Then we both go back to watching the football game.

We are both gaining weight, but missing less of the game.

Chapter 37 - January 2017

ELVIS IS IN THE BUILDING

ELVIS PRESLEY HAS got me All Shook Up.

The Chronicle editorial board meets every Wednesday to discuss the issues of the week. One Wednesday a month we meet at the old courthouse in Inverness so it's convenient for folks on the east side to meet with us.

Last week I walked into the old courthouse and there was a portrait of Elvis Presley on the wall greeting me.

"Good morning," I said to Elvis as I entered the building.

I did a double take because he appeared to wink at me.

Most readers will remember that Elvis spent a lot of time in Citrus County making the movie "Follow that Dream." The courtroom scenes were shot in the very room the Chronicle editorial board was sitting in.

Later in the meeting we had a visit from Paul Perregaux, a Citrus Hills resident who has qualified to run for the Citrus County Community Charitable Foundation board, the non-profit organization that will decide how the proceeds from the lease of Citrus Memorial Hospital will be used.

I asked Paul to give us some background on his life experience so we could let residents know why he was running for the office. The long time banker pointed out that he had an Army career before he worked for the financial industry in New England.

He noted one interesting point about his time in the military - he was once assigned a driver by the name of Elvis Presley.

And yes, it was that Elvis Presley.

"He was a very nice young man at the time," said Paul.

Later that same day, back at the Chronicle office in Meadowcrest, we had a very extraordinary visit from April Royal, the widow of Phil Royal. Again, most every resident of this community knows about the tragic death of Phil while he was participating in the annual Key Training Center fundraising run. Phil was considered the front runner to replace retiring sheriff Jeff Dawsy in the November election.

April, her sister and some friends had come to the Chronicle to say thank you for the coverage the newspaper gave to the tragic death of Phil and all of the memorials that followed.

In a truly class act, April insisted on bringing enough ice cream to treat the 100 plus employees at the newspaper.

April brought along Brelyn, the six-month old daughter of Phil and she was the definite hit of the ice cream party.

When the ice cream party was just about over I sat for a few minutes with April and we shared the very sad news of the day - Dorothy Jean Cole, the sister of Chet Cole at the Key Training Center, had died.

Chet has dedicated his life to making the Key Training Center the incredible success it has been because his personal experience with his sister Dorothy Jean. Back in the 1970s, developmental disabled citizens were denied many basic human rights and simply warehoused by the state.

Chet knew 40 years ago there was a better way to provide services and the institution of the Key Training Center grew from that passion.

And here is where Elvis comes full circle.

As we sat their talking, April Royal explained to me that Dorothy Jean's absolute favorite musician was Elvis Presley. Her residence at the

Key Center was adorned with photos and paintings of Elvis.

In July of this year, April and Phil attended the Key Center's annual auction. Phil had been on the Key Center board for 20 years and had a special relationship with Dorothy Jean Cole.

In fact, two years ago Phil wrote "Dorothy Jean is the reason I run for the Key, and I am so blessed to have met her…Seeing the joy in Dorothy's face inspires me to be more appreciative of life and grateful for God's blessings in my life."

At the July charity event what comes up for auction but a large velvet portrait of Elvis Presley. According to April, Phil took one look at Elvis and said he needed to purchase the velvet masterpiece for Dorothy Jean.

"I don't care what it cost," Phil told April. "We need to buy Elvis."

As you might guess, the Royals were the top bidders. Phil wanted to wait until after the Run for the Money to give the present to Dorothy, but fate got in the way.

Phil died during the run at a very young 47 years old. His family and our entire community have been rocked by the tragedy.

April Royal has been an incredibly strong woman during the aftermath of the tragic events. Just last week she saw the Elvis portrait at her home and decided she had to go visit Dorothy Jean. So she loaded four-month old Brelyn and Elvis into the car and went to the Key.

She presented the Elvis portrait to Dorothy as a last gift from Phil. Dorothy was delighted to spend time holding Brelyn and she had a big smile on her face.

And now, just a few days after that visit, Dorothy Jean Cole has passed away.

The irony was almost too much to comprehend.

I looked at the velvet Elvis and I swear he winked at me again.

In a very strange way, the velvet King helped me better understand what courage looks like and how precious life really is.

Chapter 38 - September 2017

DREAMS ARE NEEDED
TO GROW SKILLS

DREAMS ARE IMPORTANT.

Sometimes they help us develop skills we never thought possible.

Other times they're just dumb.

When goofing around at home recently I managed to drop my iPad on a tile floor. While the glass on the front of the computer did not crack, I heard a little tinkling sound from the inside.

As my bad luck would have it, the iPad stopped working. My work life is hooked to the little computer and I take it with me everywhere I go.

We had become dependent on each other.

The computer had all of my records, files and internet connections on it. I couldn't work without it.

From the computer's standpoint, I had the battery charger which kept the iPad alive. It couldn't work without me.

We call that joint dependency.

Because we had been together for so long, I somehow dreamed that

I had the skill to repair the broken computer. I was sure it was just a little something that popped out place and that I would be able to stick it back in.

That is the sum and total of my computer repair knowledge.

But I dreamed the repairs would be simple.

So like your typical 'I can do anything American male' working on a lawnmower that would not start, I decided to crack open the computer and fix it.

I dreamed it was just something that popped out of place.

So I opened up the little iPad (without the knowledge that any existing warranty was now totally invalid) and got to work.

I soon discovered that inside an iPad are lots of little complicated pieces that are about as thick as a sliver of paper. Some of those little slivers had become dislodged and were obviously the reason the computer was no longer working.

So I pulled the little aimless slivers out and put them on my desk. I was pretty sure I was going to be able to find the right place to put the slivers back – if I could only pick them up. I have this dexterity issue where my fingers sometimes feel like little hot dogs.

I occasionally have trouble picking up a quarter off the counter.

Those tiny computer slivers were about 1/100th the width of a quarter, so the task grew in difficulty.

But in my dreams, I could fix anything.

The two dogs laying at my feet knew something bad was going to happen so they quietly exited the office.

In a related matter, I have this allergy problem that Dr. Grillo explained to me has something to do with Cedar trees. I live in Crystal River – once the home of the largest pencil factory in Florida. That pencil factory was dependent on Cedar trees.

Hence, I live in a neighborhood that was once one of the largest Cedar tree forests in the Sunshine State.

Which is the long reason to explain why I sneeze a lot.

When I sneeze my whole body convulses and I make a very loud noise. Dogs bark when I sneeze.

And with my sneezes comes a very large exhale of air.

As the dogs somehow knew, at the very moment I was just beginning to explore my dream of becoming a computer repair technician, I sneezed.

And then I sneezed again.

And when I looked back at the desk top and my dismantled iPad, all the little pieces were gone. They were blown away in a Cedar tree induced fit.

Which explains why a few minutes later my wife walked into my office and asked me why I was crawling around under the desk.

"I'm repairing the computer," I told her. "It's a new skill I'm working on."

She has known me long enough that she didn't ask any further questions. She just walked out of the office.

Apple reports that my new iPad will be here any day.

Chapter 39 - Nov. 2017

YOU CAN'T GO HOME AGAIN

WHEN I DROVE away for the last time it finally struck me, a chapter in our family history was closing. But it was more than that.

The strings to the town I grew up in were being cut.

Earlier this week I traveled to New York and sold our family homestead.

While I have lived in Florida for the last 40 years, there was always the family home to return to. It was the rock of stability - even though it was decaying a little bit.

We had moved into the home in the early 1960s. We listened in the family room to Walter Cronkite tell us that President Kennedy had been shot. We saw man walk on the moon and we laughed together at Archie Bunker.

It was a different time.

Every home that touched our property had six or seven children. We could put together opposing baseball teams with the friends in our immediate neighborhood.

Families were always together. We never knew anyone who had divorced parents.

We never had a lot of money in our home and every kid had to have a job as soon as they were able. We all contributed part of our pay to cover the household expenses.

With seven kids, there were lots of expenses.

We had nine people in that house and only one full bathroom. We waited on line a lot and bathed at least once a week.

The plumbing never worked in the bathroom. For more than 50 years we were treated to leaking water from the second floor bath that would drip right onto the kitchen table.

My stubborn Irish father would never call a plumber. He was man enough to fix any plumbing problem and he did so on at least a dozen occasions. He tore up the wall and the pipes and for a while we were dry.

A few months later we'd be sitting around eating a Sunday dinner and the dripping would start. The water would splash right on the table.

In the early years we would all laugh and my father would get mad.

As we got older and the scenario repeated, we'd just smile to ourselves and say a little prayer to God that some things don't change.

Even after all the kids left home, my parents lived in the big house and welcomed us home for graduations, weddings and funerals. My children and grandchildren have run up and down the hallways laughing and fighting and doing what kids do best.

The family home was the place you could go back to and remember the dreams of being young. Little league games, Boy Scouts and high school dates.

The pictures still hung on the walls. The same lumpy beds still sat in our bedrooms.

But time had moved on and change had to happen. Dad had passed away last summer and Mom could no longer live in the big house on her own. Those seven children live all around the country.

Before we sold the house we called on a plumber to come make the repairs. He ripped out the bathroom wall and for a $150 part he was able to make the repairs.

It wouldn't have been right to let that plumbing leak on the nice young family that purchased our home.

We didn't know it at the time, but that house was the structure that our parents built the fundamental values of our life around. We learned to share, to be responsible and to be a loving unit of kindred spirits with genetic bonds and leaking pipes holding us together.

I walked out of that house for the last time this week. The final ties have been cut, but the lessons will always be with us.

Chapter 40 - April 13, 2018

I AM NOT A CHICKEN, BUT I CAN'T CATCH ONE

I HAVE HAD a few experiences in my life.

I was bitten by a water moccasin and spent many days in the ICU having nightmares.

I was threatened by a sheriff (not this county) and the next day had the windows shot out of my car.

Because of my job, I have met presidents, first ladies, governors and the like.

I have surfed big waves in Hawaii.

While sitting in the Tallahassee gallery of the Florida Legislature once, I had the honor of watching our own legislator stop the proceedings, grab the microphone, point directly at me and announce to one and all: "That is the editor of my newspaper and he tells lies about me."

There was light applause.

Needless to say, there have been ups and downs. But I don't frequently back down from challenges.

So with that background, I was sitting on the front steps of my nephew's home in Weeki Wachee on Easter Sunday when my 7-year-old niece Maya asked: "Have you ever caught a chicken?"

"A chicken," I asked.

"Yes, Uncle Gerry," little Maya asked. "Do you know how to catch a chicken?"

As if on queue, a flock of chickens walked by. The Mulligan family of Weeki Wachee raises chickens because they like fresh eggs.

I thought about if for a moment. I have barbecued chicken, baked chicken, had chicken on a Caesar salad and most especially eaten William Bunch's fried chicken at Oysters; but I had never actually caught a chicken.

"No Maya," I admitted. "I have never caught a chicken."

"Why not?" she asked with pure innocence.

"Because I have never seen a chicken I wanted to catch," I admitted to her.

I grew up in the crowded neighborhoods of Long Island, New York and we didn't have chickens. As a kid, I never even saw a chicken.

We had Kentucky Fried chicken, but they came in boxes.

Living in Citrus County for all these years I have seen plenty of chickens, but I never had the desire or need to catch one.

At that moment the flock of Mulligan chickens then rushed by in the other direction.

"Let me show you, Uncle Gerry," Maya said and she got up and ran after the flock.

The chickens scurried in a bunch of directions but Maya managed to corner one of them. She put her hand right above it and the chicken crouched low to the ground. Maya scooped it up in her arms and the clucking bird snuggled up to her chest.

Maya and the chicken were both smiling.

It took her about 10 seconds to complete the task.

"Now you try," she challenged.

So what the heck, a little 7-year-old can do it with ease, how hard could this be?

I tried to nonchalantly stroll over to the flock of chickens but they all ran under a boat sitting in the yard.

I snuck around the other side of the boat and tried to grab one, but the entire flock simply scooted back under the boat.

Smart little chickens.

Digging deep into my vast experience of chicken catching (none), I picked up a handful of small pebbles and threw them in the grass in attempt to confuse the birds with a potential feeding opportunity.

The chickens ran to the grass to check out the pebbles and I quickly followed. I reached down to grab one of the birds and the chicken reacted by pecking my hand.

I looked at my finger and it was bleeding.

Maya sat on the steps of the porch and giggled.

I chased the chickens back under the boat and tried again to grab the one that had just pecked me. I missed the chicken and managed to bang my head on the boat.

The flock decided I was a nuisance and they all scooted around the house.

My finger was bleeding and my head hurt. Maya walked over and wrapped her small hand around one of my fingers.

"Maybe we should play another game," she said.

My pride wounded, I reminded her "I have met a president."

Unimpressed, she reassured me "we can try again the next time you visit."

Chapter 41 - Oct. 19, 2018

~~~

FIGHTING OFF MY NEMESIS
WITH A ONE-PRONGED HOE

IF I HAD a choice, I wouldn't even hang around with me.

Last weekend was dedicated to cleaning up around the house after Hurricane Michael scared the devil out of all of us. We got flood waters in the garage and our Crystal River streets were not passable during high tide. But there was no permanent damage.

Almost.

When I decided to go under the house (we are built up 11 feet to meet the flood rules) I followed the sidewalk and was met by a visitor.

A three-and-a-half-foot water moccasin was stretched out in front of me.

As some of you might remember, I have had numerous confrontations with water moccasins over the last two years. One interaction resulted in a poisonous bite that put me in ICU at Flagler Hospital for three nights with 16 vials of anti venom pumped into me. Medical bills topped $240,000.

So on Sunday I looked down at the water moccasin on the sidewalk and he looked at me. I saw potential pain and high medical bills. He saw lunch.

My first reaction was to run like hell for safety.

The water moccasin's first reaction was to try and take a bite out of me.

He lunged and I ran.

I am thinking there must be a water moccasin restaurant menu produced each year that has my photo on the front of it.

Either that or I put off an odor that smells like a riverfront buffet to the entire cottonmouth breed.

I am an obvious food item to the slithering reptiles.

While I escaped his first lunge, I couldn't let the confrontation end. We have grandkids that visit almost every weekend and I wouldn't be able to live with myself if anyone else got bit by this aggressive intruder.

Mr. Water Moccasin slipped into a nearby bush and waited for his next opportunity to strike.

My first reaction was to douse the bush with lighter fluid and set the whole thing on fire.

First reactions are usually not good. This one was particularly bad as I could envision explaining to the insurance agent how I burned the whole house down.

Instead, I called out to my friendly neighbor — Terry — for some assistance.

Terry is a blueberry farmer in Williston and spends the weekends at the river house. He usually has a handgun in his truck, but not today.

Instead, we decided the two of us could outsmart the water moccasin and kill it. I gave Terry a shovel and I got a hoe.

The plan was that I was going to attack the tree with the hoe and Terry would whack the fleeing snake with the shovel.

While this was a strategically sound plan, Mr. Water Moccasin didn't fully agree to the details.

When I whacked the bush with the hoe, Mr. Water Moccasin pulled a fast one and decided to come back at me and attack.

Offense is the best defense — even in the world of snakes.

While I was flailing around with the hoe, I managed to break off four of the fives prongs.

I was fighting a poisonous snake with a one-pronged hoe. (That would make a great country song).

Fortunately, our fighting strategy came together at the critical moment. Terry reached around and whacked Mr. Water Moccasin right as I came down with the final thrust of my one-pronged hoe.

I stunned the snake by driving the single prong right through the back of his head.

You might think that was the happy conclusion of the confrontation, but some things are not that simple.

Mr. Water Moccasin was now attached to the one prong of my hoe but he wasn't done trying to bite us. He kept lunging toward us.

I, with my limited snake killing experience, thought I could hurry up the conclusion by striking the snake again with the hoe.

I pulled back the hoe for a second strike but along came Mr. Water Moccasin for the ride. He was unwillingly attached to the tool.

When I reached the apex of my swing, Mr. Water Moccasin broke free and sailed into the sky.

Suddenly time stood still.

Terry and I looked up into the sky and watched Mr. Water Moccasin go for a final ride.

The biggest problem with a poisonous snake flying through the air is that eventually it must come down.

Terry and I just kept looking up for what felt like 5 minutes.

And then Mr. Water Moccasin began his inevitable fall back to earth.

I believe the thought hit both Terry and I about the same time.

This flying snake might just land right on one of us and have just enough remaining energy for that final fatal bite.

We both began to whoop and holler because that's what you do when nothing else seems to matter.

The snake slammed to the ground right at Terry's feet with a thud.

Terry showed his quick blueberry farm reflexes by chopping Mr. Water Moccasin before he could move.

I chipped in and whacked him again with my one-pronged hoe.

And Terry chopped the snake again.

And again

And again.

We were breathing hard and our hearts were pounding. This round of the water moccasin confrontation was going to the good guys.

Two years and three water moccasins all with evil intent — this just doesn't seem right.

I might have to move back to Ireland where the snakes were run off by St. Patrick. Or maybe I could get Joe Meek, the incoming mayor of Crystal River, to order all snakes to exit the city limits. The city is trying to control chickens by an ordinance, why not snakes?

In the meantime, don't hang around with me. I could be dangerous to your health.

Chapter 42 - August 2019

Now even the
squirrels are bored

My favorite part of the newspaper is the 'Services Guide' – the place where you hire competent workers to complete the home projects you should have never started in the first place.

An army of squirrels had invaded the underside of our house recently because they were also going stir crazy during the COVID-19 pandemic. The squirrels spend most of their free time on Facebook, but recently decided they needed a break so they tore out a hunk of insulation under the house and then began to chew on a water pipe.

While they made a mess of things, the damage wasn't serious. I thought I could easily handle the repairs.

After buying new insulation, wrapping the pipes and getting things in place, I borrowed one of my wife's stapler guns from her art studio.

She is a glass artist and does her own framing. The industrial strength stapler gun looked like the perfect tool to reapply the final netting cover on the insulation.

As she gave me the stapler gun, my wife looked me in the eye and said: "Let me show you how this works. You must do it this way or you could injure yourself."

I did what every good husband does. I reacted with impatience, did not really listen and grunted that I understood.

I did not understand.

The stapler gun actually worked perfectly and I finished the job after putting about 250 staples into the plastic net covering.

Later in the day it was time to take the dogs for a walk. When I got to the front door, I discovered I did not have the ability to open it. I could not grip the door knob with enough strength to turn it.

My right hand no longer worked. The fingers failed to respond to instructions from the brain and sat there like over-cooked sausages.

I could not grip the dog's leash and had to use my left hand.

After walking the dogs, I was unable to use my right hand and open a bottle of Diet Dr. Pepper (otherwise known as the 'Nectar of the Gods').

Throbbing pain began to run up my arm from my now totally numb right hand. While in excruciating pain, I realized the absolutely most important goal was to not let my wife know she was right about how to use the stapler gun.

Later that evening while sitting down for dinner, I could not hold the fork with my sausage fingers.

"Why are you using your left hand to hold the fork," my wife asked.

"I am practicing in case I lose my right arm in a tennis accident," I lied.

The next morning, I was still in pain. I could not button up my own shirt.

We were cleaning up around the house and I attempted to carry a 20-pound exercise weight with my right arm. As I walked thru the door onto the outside deck, I realized I wasn't going to make it down the stairs.

In a brilliant move, I tossed the 20-pound weight over the railing to the grass below, thus saving further strain to my right hand. When I looked over the railing it became clear that I had once again miscalculated.

Our home is on the river and the ground is soft from constant saturation. The 20-pound weight was gone – it had been sucked up by the lawn and buried deep in the tundra below.

When I got downstairs my attempts to find the 20-pound weight were unsuccessful. I got on my hands and knees and tried to dig into the mud – no luck. It was gone.

Admitting defeat is not my strongpoint so I got a shovel from the garage and began to dig up the yard in search of the weight. I could only imagine a lawn mower blade getting destroyed by the weight so I was not going to let that happen.

Using a shovel with one hand is not easy.

I dug deep and finally got my hands on the weight and tried to yank it up. The hole had filled with water so I was down on my hands and knees using my injured paw to yank.

I yanked and yanked and then slid backwards and fell into the mud puddle. I was on my back and completely soaked. I could not see because my glasses were covered with mud. I had trouble cleaning them because my swollen sausage fingers still did not work.

As I lifted myself from the muddy hole I spied four squirrels watching from the deck of the house. They had tiny scraps of insulation hanging from their squirrel coats and they were giving each other high-fives while doing a squirrel happy dance.

"Mission accomplished," the lead squirrel said in squirrel talk to his happy followers. "What do you guys want to do tomorrow."

I tried to throw a handful of mud at the revelers, but my right paw hurt so much that I missed the squirrels and hit the side of the house.

I will clean that up when my hand feels better.

For the record, the Service Directory usually runs in the B section of the paper.

Chapter 43 - Nov. 10, 2019

SOMETIMES SILENCE IS
THE BEST OPTION

CITRUS COUNTY GOT the attention of the country this week and it was not a positive experience.

Possibly we as a community can learn something from what happened.

As has been reported in the Chronicle, and just about every news outlet in the country, some members of our county commission got their feathers ruffled over a library proposal to add a digital version of the New York Times to the inventory available to residents.

Commissioners Scott Carnahan and Ron Kitchen used a routine library budget presentation to create a firestorm. Commissioner Carnahan was the most flamboyant in his opposition. He said he agreed with President Trump that the New York Times was "fake news" and said "I don't want the New York Times in this county."

I am pretty sure that Commissioner Carnahan has never been a reader of the New York Times and could not identify anything specifically that he felt was fake.

No vote was taken, but the commissioners indicated they wanted the item nixed. No money was saved, because the library is a separate taxing unit the $2,700 remains in the budget.

The reaction to the emotional outburst has been overwhelming.

News stories and television reports spread like wildfire. Cable TV pundits had great fun at our expense. The theme of the reports was disturbing – this backwards Florida town wants to ban the nation's best newspaper. Surely book burning will be the next thing on our agenda.

Thousands of emails flooded into the county offices. The county telephone system was overwhelmed with calls. The county tourism office got complaints and tourists made threats to cancel their vacations here. It's hard for some of the county staff to get any real work done while dealing with the huge flow of opinions.

The executives at the county chamber and economic development offices just slumped in their chairs fearing the lost opportunity of people who don't want to be associated with us.

This newspaper – which first wrote the story about the commission decision – has been flooded with calls, complaints and emails from people wondering what the heck is going on.

And here's the rub: The whole incident was simply political grandstanding that backfired.

The Citrus County Commission has absolutely nothing to do with the contentious debate on a national level. I don't care if you are liberal, conservative or in the middle, I think we can all agree that the national debate has become more contentious and destructive than ever before.

Freedom of the press and speech are core values in America that have nothing to do with political affiliation. Our commissioners positioned themselves to object to the U.S. Constitution? Really? This is a fight you want to wage in Inverness, Florida?

Prior to this outbreak, the contentiousness of the national fight really has not impacted what goes on with local government. For the most part, people treat each other with respect even when they disagree on the issues being debated. Citrus County, and many small communities throughout the nation, have continued to get the regular work done while the guys in Washington play their games. And that has been the real strength of America for centuries – we don't need Washington to tell us how to get the roads paved, trash picked up and water pumped.

I am sure the two commissioners involved in this fiasco didn't give it much thought, but they have pulled the national debate into local government when it has no place here. That debate was felt at the Tuesday commission meeting when people complained and some said ugly things. Commissioners got shrill in their replies. Anger, distrust and embarrassment was evident everywhere.

The Citrus County Library system is an excellent example of how we do things right. We pay a separate property tax and hire a professional staff to make the decisions about programming, content and operations.

County Commissioners don't make decisions about books, newspapers or programs in the library based on the political insecurities and/or affiliations they might have.

They also don't make the decisions about what paving material the road department uses, what bullets the sheriff buys or what day the tax collector sends out her notices.

That's not their job. Staff does that work without regard to politics.

Libraries are filled with ideas – many of which may conflict with the personal beliefs of our elected officials. We don't elect county commissioners to censor information at any level. Taxpayers and library patrons are smart enough to make their own decisions. Librarians are professionals who live by an ethical code that bars political influence.

For the record, the Chronicle delivers the New York Times to many households in Citrus County. It's expensive.

For the record, the New York Times is the best newspaper in our nation.

We also deliver the Wall Street Journal, Financial Times, USA Today, Tampa Bay Times and the New York Post to readers who want to consume that information. While I like the Chronicle the best and wish every household in the county got it delivered, I understand that many people want to take advantage of the options. Freedom to digest facts and opinions is a core value of America.

Having digital versions of the Times and other publications at the library might not be good for our delivery business.

But not everything is about us. Commissioners could learn from that.

Contributions have been offered from around the county – and around the country – to get the Citrus County Library the funding it needs to get this digital service up in the library. Saving money is not an excuse. It never was.

Fortunately, three members of the county commission have been pretty silent on this issue. They can't believe the unnecessary mess that has been made by a few commissioners pandering for political support.

Commissioner Brian Coleman has asked that the issue be placed on the agenda. Without debate or justification, the commissioners should approve the library budget and go back to debating the issues they were elected to handle.

Chapter 44 - Dec. 2, 2019

HOLIDAYS WOULD BE
NOTHING WITHOUT A SNAKE

MY FATE WILL forever be tied to snakes.

As regular readers of this column may remember, I have had a few unfortunate run-ins with the poisonous snake known as the water-moccasin or cottonmouth. Scientific folks call it the Agkistrodon piscivorus.

I call it my nemesis.

Three years ago I was bitten on the foot by a water moccasin and ended up spending the next three nightsin ICU at Flagler Hospital in St. Augustine. It took 16 vials of anti-venom to insure that my exit from this earth was not prematurely rescheduled.

Last summer during one of the storms another water-moccasin visited my house in Crystal River and, despite high levels of incompetence on my part, he was vanquished.

Fast forward to Dec. 25 and our Christmas dinner in Crystal River. It was a quiet dinner as just the three of us sat down with turkey, stuffing and the traditional fixings.

Half-way through the meal the phone rang. Without giving it a thought, I answered it.

For the record, you should never answer the phone while you're eating Christmas dinner. Nothing good happens with such calls.

This call was from a kind neighbor who was walking her dog on our street.

"There is a water moccasin on the front lawn," she said. "I'm afraid it will bite a dog or one of the kids."

And then came the kicker: "I know you have a lot of experience with snakes," she said.

That's a truthful statement, but it might be more accurate to say that snakes have a lot of experience with me. They like the way I taste. Or it might be the way I smell.

This was Christmas and I was determined not to be the victim of another snake encounter. I excused myself from the Christmas table and formulated a plan as I walked down the front stairs.

Not willing to put dogs or children at risk, I marched with determination to the garage and grabbed a large and sturdy shovel. My plan began to crystalize: I was going to approach the snake with confidence and use the shovel to dispatch its head from its body in one quick motion.

And then I was going to get back to the Christmas dinner table before the gravy on my turkey got cold.

When I confronted the snake the little beast lifted his head and snarled.

With one quick aggressive motion I raised the shovel.

Actually, there may have been too much aggression.

As I brought the shovel up high and fast to slice the snake's head from its body - disaster struck.

The moment was similar to a traffic accident experience where you can see in a split-second what's going to happen yet you can't do anything to avoid the outcome.

The angle of the thrusting shovel toward the proximity of coiled snake was interrupted by one obstacle.

My head.

On the powerful upswing of the shovel I hit myself in the middle of my forehead with the handle.

You could experience the same result if you simply got a hammer and smacked yourself as hard as you could in the head.

After the self-inflicted shot to the head I stumbled backwards and almost passed out. Blood began to stream out of the wound and get into my eyes.

Before my vision was blurred by the streaming blood, I had one last look at the uninjured water moccasin.

If snakes could laugh, that was what he was doing. He was also snapping at me.

I steadied myself with the shovel, took an unobstructed jab, and chopped off his head.

By then my wife was at my side with additional implements of snake destruction and we cut him into many parts.

After cleaning myself up I returned to the Christmas dinner table.

"Gerry got the snake," my wife told our dinner partner – her 97-year-old Mom.

That's when they both looked at me and said in unison: "What happened to your head?"

The welt was growing into an official holiday lump.

"We're not talking about it right now," I said with my best Christmas smile.

For the record, the gravy was cold.

Chapter 45 - Feb. 7, 2020

POOP IN THE SHOE RETURNS

WE ARE MORE than a month into the New Year so it's only appropriate that some new Poop in the Shoe awards be given to deserving folks.

For those not familiar, my dog Hunter dreamed up the idea of the Poop in the Shoe honors after I refused to take him for a walk during a rain storm. The two-year-old Havana Silk simply went into my closet, found a pair of work shoes, and deposited his gift inside.

I put my shoes on in the dark the next morning and discovered his gift. It was fragrant.

With similar disdain, the following deserve the recognition. I checked with Hunter and he concurs.

• Poop in the Shoe to members of our state Legislature who continue to push the idea of giving bonus payments to teachers as opposed to raising teacher pay. The criteria for awarding bonus pay is impossible to get right. It places all responsibility for student and school performance on the teacher instead of giving equal recognition to the administration of the school district, the demographics of the area and the parents of the students. At least the absurd idea of factoring in a teacher's SAT scores from college has been dropped. The whole concept of bonus pay for teachers is an arrogant insult that suggests teachers are not earning their pay. School teachers don't get into the profession to get rich. The bonus idea demonstrates that some legislators just don't get it.

Poop in the Shoe to them.

• Gov. Ron DeSantis actually has earned one free shoe cleaning for his proposal to raise minimum teacher pay to $47,500 a year. Florida average teacher pay now ranks 46 out of 50 states. We want the best public school results but our pay is near the bottom. It's like going thru the drive-in at Burger King and complaining that the meal was not as good as Oscar Penn's in Inverness.

• Poop in the Shoe to the members of the county commission who continue to convince themselves that the intersection of 491 and 200 is perfect the way it is. A Chronicle poll of readers showed that 80 percent of the population wants the intersection fixed. Some of the commissioners are obviously not interested in public opinion. They know best. Poop in the shoe to them.

• Poop in the Shoe to the Ozello homeowner who played the victim after the county came in and tore down his house. For the record, the county doesn't just come in and tear down your house. It takes years of complaints and civil action by neighbors to even get the county's attention. The only way your home gets torn down is if you create a health hazard and then totally ignore all of the legal warnings sent to you by the county and the health department. There is a point where an individual's personal pursuit of happiness (ignoring the needs of neighbors and tossing legal documents in the trash) comes in conflicts with the well-being of the entire neighborhood.

The folks who live in Ozello are not the blue-bloods of West Palm Beach. But minimum health standards are necessary in a civilized society. Ignoring every complaint and legal document and then playing the victim when the bulldozers show up is baloney.

Poop in the shoe to you.

• Poop in the Shoe to the Florida Legislature for lacking the enthusiasm to pass a new tax on water extraction from our endangered springs. Currently, a bottled water company can come in and pay $115 for a consumptive use permit to extract as much water as it wants and sell it all over the country. In the meantime, the reduced flow of water in the springs of Florida is causing salt-water intrusion and expanded pollution. Not to mention that a Citrus County homeowner along the coast would pay about $115 in three months for household water consumption. A bill in the Legislature would slap a 12.5 cent tax on each gallon a water company extracted, but legislative insiders say it has almost no chance of passing.

The 12.5 cents a gallon might be a little high, but for-profit bottled-water companies should not be able to consume millions of gallons of spring water at a lower cost than the homeowner in Citrus County pays for three months of service.

Poop in the Shoe to the Legislature.

Chapter 46 - Sept. 27, 2020

—————∽∾∽—————

MAKING PUPPIES IS REAL WORK

Warning: *This column is about sex and dogs, so make sure everyone has taken their medication before reading.*

I DON'T KNOW a whole lot about animals because as a child we never had any. I grew up in a large family where pets were banned. As a child, my late Mother was attacked by a dog and scarred for life. She was deathly afraid of dogs and had no appreciation of anything that needed four-legs to get around.

It would only make sense that I would marry a woman who loves dogs and spends much of her free time spoiling them. Our house has been filled with four-legged creatures since we got married nearly four decades ago.

But that doesn't mean I know dogs. I like them, but I did not grow up with them and am still unfamiliar with their ways.

There are times I will come home from work and walk into the house and smell something good coming from the kitchen.

"That smells great," I said. "What's for dinner."

"That's for the dogs," will come the reply. "We're having pizza."

You get the picture.

Over the last few years we have shifted to a breed of dogs known as Havana Silk. They are known for being very healthy, which after 15 years of Yorkies and monthly visits to the veterinarian, sounded liked a really nice alternative.

Our oldest male is 'Hunter Springs' named after the local beach. We call him Hunter.

Last year he participated in a big dog show with other Havana Silks from around the country and won top honors. He now prefers to be called 'Top Dog' around the house.

Part of the honor of being Top Dog is that female Havana Silks from around the country want to spend some special time with him.

Hunter doesn't mind the work, but he insists that his visitors bring flowers, dog biscuits and a few special treats.

@ I must admit that my very first experience in breeding dogs was accidental and resulted in several casualties. When I went off to college I got two puppies from the pound, a male and a female. I never gave much thought to what might happen.

As luck would have it, my mother (remember, she hates dogs) made her very first trip to Florida to visit me at exactly the wrong time.

Upon her arrival at my dwelling, I looked out the window and saw her getting out of the car. It was only then that I looked down and realized I had two dogs. The introductions were going to be difficult if not impossible.

To make matters worse, at that very moment the female puppy went into heat. I had never witnessed such a thing. I didn't even know what it meant.

The male dog immediately climbed onto the female and started to do what dogs do.

I was flabbergasted and almost forgot that my dog-fearing mother was walking up the driveway.

As a novice to canine copulation, I thought I could pull them apart and throw them out the back door.

I quickly learned that is not possible.

Being a quick thinker, I ran to the kitchen and filled a pot with cold water.

Certainly cold water would force a separation of the dynamic duo.

I dumped the water on the dogs and the only response I got was very loud barking. They were still connected and totally unable to separate. They were also both pretty sure they no longer liked me.

I now had copulating dogs that were stuck together, barking, and completely soaked from my pot of water.

With pot in hand and dog-fearing mother at the front door, I did what any God-fearing American would do. I started smacking each of the dogs in the head with the empty pot.

Now they were really sure they didn't like me. They still did not separate.

I had to push the dogs aside and squeeze out the front door to greet my mother. I suggested a walk through the neighborhood would be much more fun than inspecting the house. Later that year six puppies joined the group.

@ But back to Hunter and our breeding experience this week. Once he got to meet his very first date – the lovely Charlotte – we discovered these purebred dogs had skipped the class on copulation at doggy training school.

They jumped around and barked and attempted to make puppies, but they could never get connected the way my pound puppies did 40 years prior.

After 48 hours of trying (that's right, 48 hours) the Moms decided to call in reinforcements. They called veterinarians, dog breeders, Havana Silk experts and even looked at YouTube videos on how to make it happen.

It did not happen.

By this time the pups were so tired they could hardly lift their heads. So the Moms did what any dog loving folks would do – they loaded the tired couple up and headed out to the Veterinarian School at the University of Florida.

Leave it to those Gators (which was difficult because one Mom was an FSU grad and the other a USF alum) to figure it out.

Using the best science has to offer the Havana Silks had their business done for them. The hope is that puppies will arrive later in the year.

As for Hunter's lack of experience, the UF folks suggested his next date should be with a female who has more experience in the field, if you know what I mean.

Chapter 47 - December 2020

IF YOU REMEMBER ONE THING, REMEMBER THAT PEOPLE ARE GOOD

YOU NEED TO do me a favor this morning.

Please go to a mirror in your house, look yourself in the eyes, and say: "People are good."

Now say it again. "People are good."

You want some evidence? Here goes.

About six weeks Chronicle reporter Nancy Kennedy wrote an article about a grandmother from Homosassa who was dealt a bad hand. Sandra Ingram, 66, needed some help.

Last July her daughter was diagnosed with cancer and died leaving Sandra as the only relative able to care for her two grandchildren. A short time after that a sister who lived with her also died.

Sandra, who has health problems of her own, has been a newspaper carrier for the last 30 years delivering the Chronicle and other newspapers to homes in Citrus County. That means she works 365 days a year, so you know she is tough.

She lives on property her family owns in Homosassa, but only had a small one-room trailer that was totally unsuitable to raise her grand-children. Her granddaughter had never had a bed of her own and there was no place for one in the trailer.

Sandra had never asked anyone for help, but circumstances went downhill and she asked Nancy to write the story. Sandra didn't have the housing or resources to make anything happen, but she fiercely wanted to protect her grandchildren.

Nancy wrote the story.

The response has been nothing short of incredible.

More than 500 Citrus County residents and organizations have responded.

Each day the Chronicle's mailbox was filled with cards and enve-lopes for Sandra. One reader sent $10 in cash. Another reader of the newspaper sent a check for $10,000. "This is anonymous," the check writer wrote. "I just want to help."

There were large checks and small checks. Some used a Go Fund Me account to help. By the time the counting was all done more than $70,000 in cash and contributions were made to help Sandra Ingram and her grandkids.

The community was moved by her plight. And most wanted ab-solutely no recognition for what they were giving or doing. They just wanted to help.

A retired sheriff's deputy showed up with stump grinding equip-ment and helped clean up the property. A former county commissioner who now builds homes sent over his land clearing friends to prepare the property. The guys from Henley's Grading will be there Monday to do the work at no charge.

And then there was the gregarious restaurant owner from Crystal River who made a phenomenal gesture. The fisherman turned res-taurant owner wanted to lead the effort to buy a new mobile home and put it on the property in the Homosassa. (He doesn't want to be identified, but his name is Jimmy Stoltz over at Seafood Cellar – I just can't help myself).

He found one over at Gainey Custom Modular and Manufactured Homes in Homosassa and owner Matt Gainey agreed to give him a really good price.

Then the folks with Withlacoochee River Electric Co-op Operation Round-Up program stepped up and pledged another $10,000 contribution to help pay for a portion of the new mobile home.

And then county commissioner Jeff Kinnard heard there were some obstacles with permits for quickly making all these improvements and he got involved. County administrator Randy Oliver and the county permit staff got on board and helped Sandra navigate the permit process and make everything legal.

And then another senior citizen knocked on the door of the Chronicle's office in Meadowcrest and wanted to give another $10,000 toward the effort.

There is a lot of anger and hate being knocked around in our country these days fueled by the national election. Some people wonder if we can, as a nation, survive the turmoil.

But then along comes a community like Citrus County where people were asked to focus on the plight of a grandmother in need. Forget about Republicans, Democrats, and COVID and the economy. Everyone just came together and helped turn one family's tragedy into a mission of hope.

Sandra Ingram and her two grandchildren are about to get a new home on a pretty piece of property. They're going to have some money together to prepare for the future. That little granddaughter is going to have a bed to sleep in.

You know why this happen?

Because people are good.

Say that one more time in the mirror for me. "People are good."

Chapter 48 - Jan. 17, 2021

———

TOMMY LASORDA BLED
BLUE AND LOVED JAZZ

BACK IN THE day, I was in Crystal River walking across the campus of the Plantation Inn. As I entered the double doors of the main registration area, I noticed someone coming up right behind me.

I politely held the door open for him, looked into his face, and realized he was the famous Major League baseball manager Tommy Lasorda.

Lasorda was the manager of the Los Angeles Dodgers for twenty years and a member of the Baseball Hall of Fame. He twice skippered the Dodgers to World Series victories - the guy was famous.

I instinctively knew that Lasorda was in town at the invitation of Ted Williams, the baseball great who lived in Citrus Hills. Every years Williams would induct Major League ball players into his Hitters' Hall of Fame and Citrus County filled up with famous sports people.

They would come to our town, play golf, and reminisce about the good old days.

"Welcome to Crystal River Mr. Lasorda," I said to him as I held the door open. I was at the Plantation for a civic meeting and had a name tag on that clearly said "Gerry Mulligan."

As a baseball fan I was delighted to be standing there with the famous Tommy Lasorda. I was stammering and tried to ask him some relevant question, but I was intimidated by this baseball great.

The famous manager then looked at my name tag. Then he looked into my face. "You're Gerry Mulligan! I love your music."

He then turned to some other ballplayers gathered in the Plantation Inn foyer and announced "This is Gerry Mulligan guys. He is the greatest saxophone player of all time."

Talk about uncomfortable moments. I would have loved to hang around with famous baseball players, drink beer and tell stories, but I was not that Gerry Mulligan.

Gerry Mulligan was a top-ranked American Jazz Saxophonist. He played with famous jazz musicians like Chet Baker, Thelonious Monk, Stan Getz, Miles Davis and Dave Brubeck.

He won a Grammy Award in 1981 and was praised as the greatest jazz baritone of all time.

He was born in New York City, as was I.

He had a close cut beard and had Irish skin damaged by the sun. So do I.

He was really handsome and you all know the similarities there.

He was one of the greatest musicians of all time.

I, on the other hand, am not permitted to sing in the shower. My wife says it scares the dogs.

My voice is so bad that grandchildren have been known to cover their ears when I sing.

I started a rock-and-roll band when I was 13-years old and at our very first (and only) engagement they paid us if we promised to stop playing.

I was not the famous Jazz musician Gerry Mulligan. I have zero talent.

Tommy Lasorda was not hearing any of it.

"You've got to play something for us," Tommy said and all his baseball player friends standing in the foyer agreed. "Where's your Sax?

"Mr. Lasorda," I said. "I am not that Gerry Mulligan.

"You are the best ever," he replied. "We must hear you play."

"I can't do it," I insisted.

"I have always wanted to hear you play," he pleaded.

I was not going to win this argument. Tommy Lasorda was one of the best baseball managers of all time and he had honed his arguing skills with the best major league umpires in baseball.

He knew how to win. He knew how to argue.

He was not going to let me go.

"I will go to my car and get the sax," I finally told him in resignation. "Why don't you guys get a seat in the bar and I will be back in a minute.

He was delighted. Tommy Lasorda and the other players went to the bar and ordered a beer.

I went back into the parking lot, got in my car, and drove away.

I never saw Tommy Lasorda again.

Tommy Lasorda died last Thursday in California. He was 93 and one of the greatest baseball managers who ever lived. He bled the Dodger blue, staying with the team for his entire career.

He loved jazz. And Gerry Mulligan.

And he knew how to win an argument.

RIP.

Chapter 49 - March 14, 2021

———— ❧ ————

BE AFRAID, BUT DON'T
BE FRIGHTENED

Editor's note: *This is a question raised by a reader of the Chronicle this week. After being published, the column was picked up by news services and republished in newspaper's around the country.*

Mr. Mulligan, I always feel that you're an honest and intelligent man. You don't show partiality toward any political party. My concern and my worry is that with all the changes that these people in Congress made, will this still be a free America like we were used to and that the country was founded on? I find some of the letters in the Chronicle that the people write in unfortunate. I can't email something in, but maybe you could answer this simple question: I'm not a young girl anymore, but I would love the United States to stay free. My husband fought for it in Vietnam. My father fought for it in World War II – proud Americans. But it looks like some of the things that are going on are changing our country. This is a proud country with proud people. Please see if you can come up with an answer that might help me and a lot of other people that are worried. I know your answer is going to be bipartisan and not prejudiced. If you can't answer, it is understandable, but I do look forward to you because I find you're intelligent and fact-checkable. You check before you say; you seek facts before you speak and you don't make up stories. I don't want it sugarcoated. I'm frightened, I very frightened that we won't be free in a few years and I'm not young enough to stand through it. I just had to ask you because I do feel confident in all your commentaries and your answers whenever you can. Thank you again and stay strong and bipartisan and true to your word, as you are.

And my answer:

Dear reader: Be afraid, but not frightened.

Be afraid that there are some folks in our country who are so self-righteous in their hatred that they will compromise the very foundations of our republic to achieve their short term political goals.

But don't be frightened, because there are far more good and reasonable people in our nation who place high value on the institutions and constitutional structure that makes us the greatest nation on earth. The good people far out-number the radicals on both sides of the political spectrum. The majority of our citizens are not willing to sell out.

Be afraid of people who tell you that only Democrats are correct or that only Republicans have the righteous answers.

But don't be frightened because the majority of Americans, the good and decent people of this nation, understand that both political parties filter the truth to fit their narrative. They are both skewed – and deep down we all know it. There are good and decent people on both sides of the debate, but neither faction has the franchise on truth.

Be afraid of the national news media that pretends to present you the truth through a biased filter in hopes of creating huge like-minded audiences so they can make millions for themselves and their corporations.

But don't be frightened because we know that the news presented by the profit-crazed entities such as MSNBC, FOX News, CNN and others is not really news – it is mostly opinion about the news. It belongs in the same category as your brother-in-law at Thanksgiving dinner telling everyone what's wrong with the country. The right response is: "Please pass the turnips." The local news media – like this newspaper – are part of the towns and cities where they reside. If they get off track (and we all do on occasion) the community will let us know about it.

Be afraid that some people are so radicalized that they believe they have the right to storm the U.S. Capitol, create mayhem, and injure the people inside.

But don't be frightened because the majority is outraged and embarrassed by the thugs. Real Americans know that change happens thru elections. Laws are changed by the legislative process and challenged in the courts. The process might be slow at times, but it is the best ever created. Thugs are losers and they go to jail.

Be afraid that some alleged demigods want to control the country by creating fear and hatred among the population.

But don't be frightened because America is not made up of unknown people. We know these people because they are us.

There are 19,495 small towns in America. There are another 310 cities with populations over 100,000 people.

In each one of those towns and cities there are good people like Joe Meek who serves as the Mayor of Crystal River. Their schools are run by people like our Sam Himmel and Thomas Kennedy. And they have their own Ruthie Davis Schlabach and Jeff Kinnard steering their counties. They have law enforcement agencies managed by people like Mike Prendergast. They have leaders like Mayor Bob Plaisted and council member Cabot McBride in Inverness.

Each of those places have libraries and churches and food banks. The have business communities that have leaders like Josh Wooten and

Ardath Prendergast. They have Boy Scouts, YMCA's and Boys and Girls Clubs. There are small businesses, little league teams and dance lessons.

Don't be frightened because together we are the backbone of America. There are 19,805 places just like our community.

We may root for different ball teams, elect people from another political party and attend different churches. But at the end of the day, we have much more in common with each other than you can ever imagine.

We all value our freedom and the basic foundations of our form of government. We will disagree about the specifics of how we are governed. We will argue with passion. But we will not forfeit our collective right to govern ourselves.

We don't know each other's names, but they are just like us.

Be afraid.

But don't be frightened.

We will climb out of our current problems because that is what we do. And we will be free.

Chapter 50 - June 26, 2001

FATHER USED TO KNOW BEST

Many of us grew up with a television show titled "Father Knows Best."

It starred Robert Young, Lauren Chaplin and Jane Wyatt and ran from 1954 to 1960.

In 2021, you could be arrested if you even said "Father Knows Best" aloud.

Today is officially Father's Day so just maybe we get some special dispensation for the weekend. But the little secret is that women have known for generations that Fathers don't really know best. Many women let their husbands live with that delusion, but the world has changed.

Men are not really in charge. If we were, we would have to take sole responsibility for the mess we've made of this place.

If Father's knew best, would I have all these issues?

- I cannot make the remote control for the television work. I am notified once a month via a bill that we have something called Netflix, but I could never actually watch anything on Netflix unless my wife was in the room.

- I cannot make oatmeal. When the grandchildren say they would like oatmeal for breakfast, I make believe I cannot hear them. Furthermore, I have never actually tasted oatmeal.
- I cannot change out the fire alarms in the house. When the batteries die, I take down the beeping alarm and bury it in the backyard. Please do not tell my insurance agent.
- I cannot tell the difference between the washing machine and the dryer because I have never personally turned them on. When a repairman showed up one day to fix the dryer, I pointed him to the washing machine. He just shook his head and gave a sympathetic look toward my wife.
- I cannot stop my cell phone from butt dialing other people. I once accidentally butt dialed the White House. Apparently, Jimmy Carter no longer lives there.
- I cannot catch a fish. As a kid, my older brother hooked me in the back with his fishing hook requiring a hospital visit and several stitches to put me back together. Every time I try to fish, my back begins to twitch.
- I cannot eat Brussels sprouts. I have a gag reflex that instantly becomes activated when I try. I do not even understand why people would want to eat Brussels sprouts.
- I cannot speak French. I took French in high school because everyone else was taking Spanish. I failed French every semester and even went to summer school because I was so bad. The French teacher told me to take Spanish. She actually begged me to take Spanish.
- I cannot say "no" to grandchildren. I said "no" to our own children fifty times a day, but I am incapable of saying it to the members of the next generation. Something in my brain has malfunctioned.
- My wife has her own buzz saw, chain saw, welding gun, glass

kiln, electric weed-whacker, blower, dremel, grinder, mosaic cutter, sander, pliers, 27 screwdrivers, socket wrenches, electric drill, cutting tables and a workshop.

I have a hammer.

She does almost all of the work around the house. I am called when a hammer is needed. Or when a fire alarm needs to be buried in the backyard.

Father Knows Best, but women are usually the ones who get the job done. I'm waiting for the updated television show to point that out. Of course, to watch the show my wife will have to be in the room to make the remote work.

CPSIA information can be obtained
at www.ICGtesting.com
Printed in the USA
LVHW100740211122
733499LV00016B/1229